EDITOR: LEE JOHNSON

MEN-AT-ARMS

THE OTTOMAN 1914

Text by
DAVID NICOLLE PhD
Colour plates by
RAFFAELE RUGGERI

First published in Great Britain in 1994
by Osprey, an imprint of Reed Consumer Books Limited,
Michelin House, 81 Fulham Road,
London SW3 6RB
and Auckland, Melbourne, Singapore and Toronto

© 1994 Reed International Books Limited

All rights reserved. Apart from any fair dealing for the purpose of private study, research, criticism or review, as permitted under the Copyright Designs and Patents Act, 1988, no part of this publication may be reproduced, stored in a retrieval system, or transmitted in any form or by any means, electronic, electrical, chemical, mechanical, optical, photocopying, recording or otherwise, without the prior permission of the copyright owner. Enquiries should be addressed to the Publishers.

ISBN 1 85532 412 1

Printed in Hong Kong

Dedication
For Giovanni Merlo,
whose love of the subject made this book possible.

Publisher's Note
Readers may wish to study this title in conjunction with the following Osprey publications:
  MAA123 *The Australian Army at War, 1899–1975*
  MAA208 *Lawrence and the Arab Revolts*
  MAA 80 *The German Army 1914–1918*
  MAA 81 *The British Army 1914–1918*
  Campaign 8 *Gallipoli 1915*

For a catalogue of all books published by Osprey Military please write to:

The Marketing Manager,
Consumer Catalogue Department,
Reed Consumer Books,
Michelin House, 81 Fulham Road,
London SW3 6RB

THE OTTOMAN ARMY 1914-18

INTRODUCTION

The Ottoman Turkish Empire was one of the leading protagonists in the First World War of 1914–18, and the stolid courage of the individual Ottoman soldier – 'Johnny Turk', as he was to his enemies, was recognized by all. Yet the army in which Johnny Turk served is, like the Ottoman Empire itself, generally little understood. The Empire had already been in existence for six centuries and was still a formidable force. Although it was apparently tottering towards its final collapse, it was not, as is so often thought, already finished.

Over the four years of the 'Great War', the Ottoman Army, Navy and two tiny air services fought on five major fronts (Gallipoli, Sinai-Palestine, Arabia, Iraq and the Caucasus). Ottoman troops also served in many other war zones (Romania, Galicia, on the Eastern front, the Salonika front, Libya, Arabia, Yemen and Iran). In addition, Ottoman agents stirred up trouble for the Allies, much further afield, in the French Saharan territories, Sudan, Ethiopia, Somalia, Oman, Afghanistan, Russian Central Asia and even the East Indies – no small feat for an Empire which had been called the 'Sick Man of Europe' for almost a hundred years!

The Ottoman Army of the Great War, is, like the Ottoman Empire itself, often wrongly seen as being entirely dominated by Imperial Germany. Most works on the Ottoman Army of the period were written by German officers and advisors; few Turkish accounts have been translated into Western languages and as a result the Ottoman Army has too often been seen as little more than an extension of the Imperial German Army. This was far from true: the foundations of the Ottoman Army remained Turkish and Islamic, as did the attitudes and aspirations of most of its officers and men. Of course German influence was strong, especially after Germany won a concession to build the famous 'Berlin to Baghdad' railway, but this aspect must not be allowed to obscure the important independent role that the Ottoman Empire played in the Great War. The Ottoman government maintained its own war policies which conflicted in many ways with those of Germany.

The Ottoman Turks had recently been virtually

Cemal Paşa at his headquarters on the Palestine front, conferring with his Chief of Staff, Colonel Ali Fuat Bey. On the left is his ADC, a naval officer, and a Circassian bodyguard with traditional cartridge pockets on the breast of his tunic and a long dagger in his belt. (Imperial War Museum Q45339)

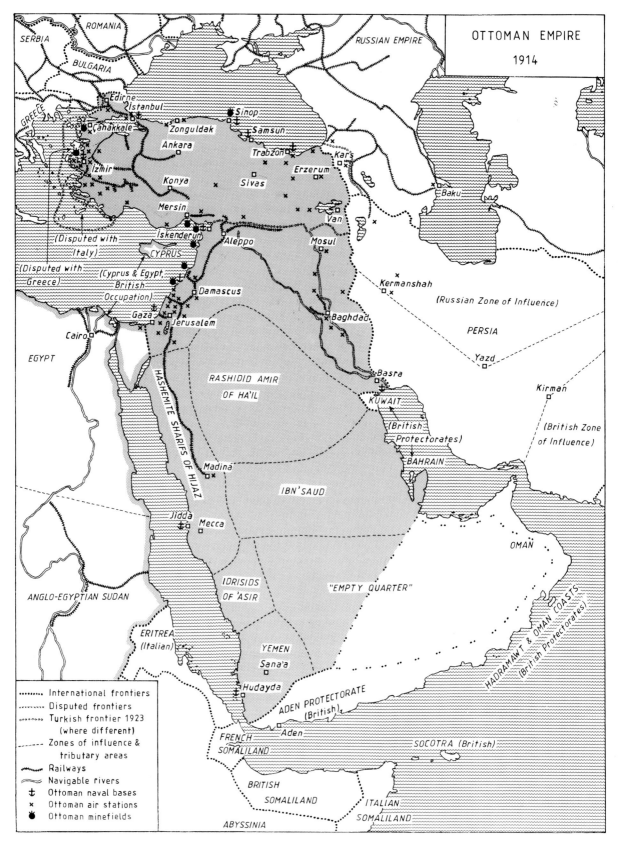

driven out of Europe in the First Balkan War (1912–13) fought against Serbia, Bulgaria and Greece. But the Empire still held huge territories in Asia including almost all of the Arab Middle East, and these the Ottomans were determined to keep. They also had their eyes on the vast, ethnically Turkish lands in the Caucasus and Central Asia. Lying behind the apparently reckless Ottoman decision to enter the Great War was a dream of imperial revival – of a new pan-Turkish empire in the east to be carved out at Russia's expense.

PRELUDE TO THE GREAT WAR

In 1908–9 a revolution led by army officers overthrew Sultan Abdülhamit II, the last autocratic absolute ruler of the Ottoman dynasty, and although Ottoman sultans remained on the throne for another 14 years, real power fell to the Committee of Union and Progress, the so-called 'Young Turks'. Rule was shared between Talat Paşa as Minister of the Interior, Enver Paşa as Minister of War and Chief of the General Staff, and Ahmet Cemal Paşa as Minister of Marine – a triumvirate which soon became a shared dictatorship.

The 'Young Turk' revolution ignited a period of violent upheaval. At the same time reforms were made in most aspects of the Ottoman state; these were barely underway before the Ottoman Empire faced blatant aggression from Italy in Libya, followed by two Balkan Wars. The year 1914 saw the Empire shorn of almost all its European territory, and effectively reduced to Anatolia and the Arab provinces. Not only were large numbers of Balkan Muslims massacred in these wars but the now shrunken Ottoman Empire had to absorb a massive influx of refugees fleeing various spates of 'ethnic cleansing' by Greeks, Serbians, Montenegrans and Bulgarians. During these bitter years the new 'nationalist' ideology of Pan-Turkism gained support among the Turkish majority population of the Empire.

Immediately after the catastrophic Balkan Wars the Ottoman government turned for support to Britain and the other entente powers, France and

Officer cadet, Feyzi Mengüç. Apart from the new kalpak lamb's wool hat, the uniform worn by cadets seems to be closer to that of the Ottoman officer corps as a whole before the changes introduced by the Young Turks Revolution. (Askeri Müzesi, Istanbul)

Russia; but this was denied, and the Young Turks had to fall back on Germany. Russia's ambitions in eastern Anatolia were, however, opposed by the other powers. Naturally they were seen by the Ottoman government as the first steps towards the annexation of the eastern provinces. Nevertheless, the Ottoman Army gained valuable experience in these troubled years, particularly in defence of the Libyan coast against Italian naval attack – experience which was to be put to good effect at Gallipoli four years later.

Army Reforms

During its decadent period in the 19th century, the Ottoman Empire had often tried to reform its armed forces by hiring European officers. At the time of the Crimean War there had been strong French influence, but by the late 19th century the Army was modelling itself almost entirely upon German lines. This was largely the result of a number of German military missions, chiefly those of Von der Goltz (1886–1895) and Liman von Sanders (1913–1918). Abdülhamit II favoured German advisors and German armaments for the simple reason that Germany seemed to have fewer vested interests in the Middle East. The importance of these missions can hardly be overestimated, especially in the education of a new class of junior and middle ranking officers, both Turkish and Arab, who would make their mark during the First World War.

Sultan Abdülhamit II (1876–1909) had taken a keen interest in his Army and, in particular, had made great efforts to make conscription fairer: all Muslim males became eligible except those from the traditionally exempted areas of Istanbul, Albania, Najd and Hijaz in Arabia, Tripoli and Benghazi in Libya, together with a number of nomad groups. Students in higher education were also exempt for the term of their studies. Muslim refugees from European persecution now became an important source of educated and highly motivated recruits. Under the new con-

Above: Şevki Bey, CO of 15th Army Corps in Galicia photographed on 11 September 1916. Ottoman troops sent to support the Germans and Austro-Hungarians on the Eastern front were something of an elite. Their kit was, at first, the best available. (Askeri Müzesi, Istanbul)

Left: Turkish infantry awaiting the first Allied landings on the Gallipoli peninsula. Most still wear the white summer uniforms that were being phased out as the Great War began. Equally obvious is the lack of defensive trenches in this sector.

Ottoman infantry encamped at Beersheba in southern Palestine in October 1917. Note the multi-racial nature of the troops. (Copyright Westminster Dragoons Museum Trust; photograph supplied by the National Army Museum, London)

scription system a man served only three years on active duty, much less than in the past, followed by six years in the *ihtiyat* active reserve, nine in the *redif* inactive reserve and two in the *mustahfiz* homeguard.

However, improvements to the Ottoman Army were more obvious in the European than in the Asian provinces, which remained somewhat backward and even retrograde. Under the despotic rule of Sultan Abdülhamit II, energetic young officers were often objects of suspicion. During the final years of Abdülhamit's reign reforms were neglected, and no large military manoeuvres were held. Consequently the Army lacked training and capable senior officers until the revolution of 1909.

After 1909 increasingly urgent efforts were made to modernize the Army and the Navy, and much new equipment was ordered. A military advisory council drew up new administrative systems and despite the opposition of a conservative bureaucracy, the Army reserves were reorganized. Medical and veterinary services were created along with new training centres, the most effective being those for NCOs and infantry riflemen. More revolutionary were the new conscription laws which declared for the first time that all the sultan's subjects, including non-Muslims, were liable for military service.

First Balkan War

Despite the Young Turks' best endeavours much of the Army had yet to be trained to use its new equipment when four Balkan states turned on the Ottoman Empire, prompting the First Balkan War of 1912–13. Despite minor success in regaining Edirne in the Second Balkan War of 1913, the previous overwhelming defeat of Ottoman arms made the case for military reform indisputable. German officer advisors were now given greater scope, the old Imperial Arsenal in Istanbul was modernized and new military factories established. Hundreds of senior officers were retired, and replaced by younger, German-trained men.

In December 1913 the most famous of all German advisors arrived in Istanbul – Liman von Sanders, a member of a converted Prussian Jewish family, and a man who was to prove his military skill against the British in Gallipoli and Palestine. Von Sanders and about 40 other Germans took service in the Ottoman Army in the winter of 1913–14 to further reorganize and reform the Sultan's troops, but their efforts made little progress before the Great War engulfed the region.

The outbreak of World War One

On 4 April 1914 Talat Paşa, Minister of the Interior, said that Turkey was like a man attacked by robbers in a forest. Such a man, he said, would happily give up his money, his goods, even his clothes if only his life and perhaps his shirt was spared. Less than three months later a Serbian terrorist gunned down an

NCOs training with a large wooden grenade-throwing catapult. Naval as well as Army personnel appear in another photograph taken at the same time, indicating that part of the Ottoman Navy was involved in coastal defence. (Askeri Müzesi, Istanbul)

Austrian archduke in Bosnia and the world was driven towards the worst war it had yet known. On 1 August, even as the war clouds gathered, German and Ottoman representatives proposed that the Ottoman Empire muster an army of 120,000 men in Thrace, ready for a joint Ottoman-Bulgarian attack on southern Russia, with another force of 90,000 troops available a month later. The following day Germany and the Ottoman Empire signed a secret alliance, though this did not commit the Ottomans to declaring immediate war on Germany's enemies. Acutely aware of its military weakness, the Ottoman government remained neutral for several months after the outbreak of war, the only member of the ruling 'Young Turk' triumvirate to favour action being Enver Paşa. A Turkish colonel was also sent to Sofia to discuss a possible pact with Bulgaria against a feared Serbian-Greek alliance.

The narrow straits that linked the Aegean Sea to the Black Sea – the Dardanelles in the south and the Bosphorus in the north – were among the most strategically important waterways in the world. They also led directly to the Ottoman capital of Istanbul. Not surprisingly, the Ottoman Navy laid a minefield to protect the Dardanelles as early as 3 August.

For several years the Ottoman government had been making efforts to strengthen the ill-equipped and outgunned Ottoman Navy. Two modern battleships, the *Sultan Osman I* and the *Resadiye* partly paid for by public subscriptions, had been ordered from British shipyards and were nearing completion when the Great War started. The British Admiralty's seizure of these ships for the Royal Navy had a devastating impact in Istanbul, even among pro-British groups. Within a few days two large German warships, the cruisers *Goeben* and *Breslau*, arrived off the Dardanelles seeking sanctuary from a pursuing British fleet. They were permitted to enter Ottoman waters where they were soon transferred, by a fictitious sale, to the Ottoman Navy, becoming the battlecruiser *Sultan Selim Yavuz* (normally shortened to *Yavuz*) and the light cruiser *Midilli*. Their crews put on Ottoman uniform and their commander, Admiral Souchon, became head of the Ottoman Navy.

British vessels patrolling off the Dardanelles then gave notice that henceforth any warships venturing into the Aegean Sea would be regarded as hostile. The Ottoman Navy promptly closed the straits to foreign shipping and laid further mines. Even so the Ottoman Empire remained neutral, until 29 October 1914, when the *Yavuz*, *Midilli* and other Ottoman warships suddenly opened fire on Russian naval bases in the Black Sea.

Though it is unlikely that the Ottoman Empire's strategically important position would have allowed it to remain neutral for long, the reasons for the attack on Russia are still a matter of debate. The main responsibility lay with Enver Paşa, supported by a pro-German faction within the ruling Committee of Union and Progress. But it is not even certain that the Germans wanted such precipitate action by a militarily weak ally at such an early point in the war. In the end the bombardments were made on the authority of Enver Paşa as Minister of War, without the knowledge or consent of the Sultan's Grand Vizier and most other government ministers. Yet doubts remained almost to the last moment.

The German crews of the *Yavuz (Goeben)* and *Midilli (Breslau)* would naturally do what they were ordered, but would Turkish Naval officers, many of whom had been trained by the British, take such controversial orders from a German admiral? On 29 October 1914 the die was cast and the Ottoman Navy shelled several Russian Black Sea ports, following an almost certainly false claim that a Russian ship had been caught trying to mine the entrance to the Bosphorus. On 2 November, Russia declared war on the Ottoman Empire, followed three days later by Britain and France. Even before this, British ships had sunk an Ottoman minelayer in the Gulf of Izmir and bombarded Aqaba in the Red Sea. The shelling of the Dardanelles fortresses by an Anglo-French fleet on 3 November merely confirmed that the Ottomans were now at war with the world's three largest empires.

A conference on 1 August between Ottoman and German representatives had proposed that the Ottomans adopt a strictly defensive posture toward the Russians on the Caucasus front while seizing naval domination of the Black Sea. But all such plans were academic while the positions of Bulgaria and Romania remained undecided. Meanwhile Germany's Austro-Hungarian allies got into difficulty on the Galician front and requested an urgent Ottoman seaborne invasion of the Ukraine to divert the Russians. The German High Command, however, preferred an Ottoman strike against the Suez Canal to disrupt Britain's communications with its Indian Empire. The Germans also promised the Ottomans huge territories in the Russian-ruled Caucasus and Central Asia, not to mention neutral Iran. In the event the plan to attack the Suez Canal won the day and the invasion of the Ukraine was called off.

The outbreak of war was greeted in Istanbul with deep gloom. Cavit Paşa, one of four ministers to resign in disgust at their country's entry into the war, declared: 'It will be our ruin – even if we win.' For the remainder of the war, real power was to stay locked in

A Turkish soldier on guard in the snow of the Eastern Front, Galicia 1916. He wears the huge shaggy fur coat used by eastern Anatolian peasants since at least the 6th century, as well as large fur over-boots. (Askeri Müzesi, Istanbul)

the hands of Enver, Talat and Cemal. Enver Paşa ran the Ottoman war effort almost single-handedly as a military dictator; Cemal Paşa took control of Syria and became its effective ruler; and Talat Paşa concentrated on civil matters in the capital. Provincial governors ran their regions with differing degrees of autonomy and apparently differing enthusiasm for the war. In Izmir, for example, Rahmi Bey behaved almost as if his province was a neutral zone between the warring states.

Finally, of course, the entire Ottoman state was defeated in 1918. This effectively signalled the end of the ancient Ottoman Empire though its last vestiges were not buried until the declaration of the Turkish Republic in 1923.

CHRONOLOGY

The Ottoman Army fought on several fronts during the First World War. Events in one region naturally affected those elsewhere, but poor communications within the Empire meant that the Turks were often fighting three or four separate wars.

1914

2 Aug.	Ottoman-German treaty of alliance.
11 Aug.	German warships *Goeben* & *Breslau* reach Turkey.
September	Russia seizes control of north-west Iran.
26 Sept.	Britain declares Ottoman warships outside the Dardanelles hostile.
28–9 Oct.	Ottoman Navy bombards Russian bases in Black Sea.
November	British Navy bombards Yemen coast.
1 Nov.	Russian troops invade eastern Turkey.
2–5 Nov.	Russia, Britain & France declare war on Ottoman Empire.
14 Nov.	Sultan declares *Jihad* against Russia, Britain & France.
22 Nov.	British occupy Basra in southern Iraq.
30 Nov.	Ottomans invade British-occupied Egypt.
December	Ottoman offensive against Russians on Caucasus front results in disaster.
Winter 1914–15	Britain occupies Aegean islands outside Dardanelles.

1915

January	Ottomans enter Tabriz in north-west Iran after Russian withdrawal & attempt to take oil-fields in south-west Iran.
2–3 Feb.	Ottoman attempt to cross Suez Canal fails.
19 Feb.	Allied (British & French) Navies bombard Dardanelles.
4 Mar.	Allied marine landing on Gallipoli Peninsula driven off.
18 Mar.	Allied (British & French) Navies attempt to break through Dardanelles, driven off with heavy loss.
28 Mar.	Russian Navy bombards Turkish ports in Black Sea, further bombardments later in year. Ottoman forces in Yemen invade British-ruled Aden Protectorate.
April	Armenian rebels seize Van in eastern Anatolia, British occupy oil-fields in south-west Iran.
25 Apr.	Allied landings on Gallipoli Peninsula & Asiatic shore of Dardanelles.
May	Russian advance in eastern Anatolia reaches Lake Van, reoccupy north-west Iran. British begin advance up Tigris in Iraq.
July	Ottomans defeat British force outside Aden.
August	Ottoman forces retake Van from Russians & Armenians.

Flag medals ceremony at Medina in the Hijaz, 1917. The long ribbons being tied to the top of the flagpole represent gallantry awards given to the unit as a whole. (Askeri Müzesi, Istanbul)

Cavalry recruited from the Turkish parts of the Ottoman Empire riding through Beersheba on their way to the southern Palestine front in April 1917. The men wear assorted kabalak *hats while their officer has an altogether finer uniform. But all ride small horses or ponies. (Imperial War Museum Q72744)*

6 Aug.	Additional Allied landings on Gallipoli Peninsula.
29 Sept.	British occupy Kut in Iraq.
22–25 Nov.	Ottomans defeat British at battle of Ctesiphon in Iraq, British retreat towards Kut.
7 Dec.	Ottomans besiege British in Kut.

1916

8 Jan.	Final Allied withdrawal from Gallipoli Peninsula.
14 Jan.	Start of large Russian offensive on Caucasus front.
15 Feb.	Fall of Erzerum to Russians.
18 Apr.	Russians seize Trabzon on Black Sea coast.
29 Apr.	British surrender at Kut.
6 May	Ottoman combined operation retakes Uzun island in Aegean from British.
May–June	Ottoman counter-offensive in eastern Anatolia.
27 Jun.	Arab Revolt against Ottoman Empire proclaimed in western Arabia.
July	Renewed Russian offensive in eastern Anatolia.
August	Small Ottoman counter-offensive in eastern Anatolia.
4 Aug.	Ottoman thrust across Sinai Pensinula defeated at Romani.
Summer	Ottoman Expeditionary Force is sent to help Germans, Austro-Hungarians & Bulgarians in the Balkans & on the Eastern Front.
18 Sept. & 3 Nov.	Ottoman naval raids against Greek 'pirate' islands off Aegean & Mediterranean coasts.

1917

Winter	Outbreak of typhus on Caucasus front.
25 Feb.	British retake Kut in Iraq.
March	Russian Revolution, Russian Army ceases offensive operations.
10–11 Mar.	British occupy Baghdad.
26–27 Mar.	Ottomans defeat British at First Battle of Gaza.
April	Russian Army starts retreat from eastern Anatolia.
19 Apr.	Ottomans defeat British at Second Battle of Gaza.
25 Jun.	Last Ottoman-Russian naval clash in the Black Sea.
Summer	Creation of new Yıldırım Army intended to reconquer Iraq from British.
6 Sep.	Huge explosion in Istanbul destroys much of Yıldırım Army's equipment.
31 Oct.	British defeat Ottomans at Third Battle of Gaza.
December	Ottoman & German naval blockade imposed on Russian Black Sea coast.
8 Dec.	British occupy Jerusalem.
18 Dec.	Ceasefire agreed between Ottomans & newly independent Transcaucasian Republic (Armenia, Azarbayjan & Georgia).
28 Dec.	Armistice signed at Brest-Litovsk ends fighting between Ottoman & Russian forces.

Ottoman Arab cavalry on their way to a military review in Damascus, April 1917. Other photographs taken on the same occasion show that they were accompanied by a 'dervish' band. (Imperial War Museum Q107326)

1918

20 Jan.	Large Ottoman naval raid into Aegean from Dardanelles.
21 Feb.	British occupy Jericho.
26–31 Mar.	Ottomans defeat British in First Battle of Amman.
26 Apr.	Ottomans retake Kars on Caucasus front.
30 Apr–3 May.	Ottomans defeat British in Second Battle of Amman.
May–June	Transcaucasian Republic fragments into three states (Armenia, Georgia, Azarbayjan)
28 Jun.	Death of Sultan Mehmet V, succeeded by Mehmet VI.
August	British occupy Baku oil-fields on Caspian coast.
14 Sep.	Ottomans & Azarbayjan forces drive British from Baku oil-fields.
17 Sep.	Troops of Arab Revolt sever Ottoman communications on Palestine front.
19 Sep.	British break through Ottoman front in Palestine.
1 Oct.	Troops of Arab Revolt occupy Damascus.
25 Oct.	British occupy Aleppo.
30 Oct.	Ottoman government signs Armistice with Allies at Mudros. Followed by occupation of most of Anatolia & Thrace by British, French, Italian & Greek forces.

1919

January	Ottoman garrison in Medina finally surrenders to forces of Arab Revolt.
April	Beginning of Turkish 'War of Liberation' against Allied armies of occupation in Anatolia.

THE ARMY

The Ottoman Army was mobilized in August 1914, immediately after war broke out in Europe, and three Armies were established. The First and Second were based west and east of the capital Istanbul, while the Third faced the Russian frontier in the Caucasus. In November 1914, after the Ottomans entered the war, a Fourth Army was created in Syria. A Fifth Army was established in the spring of 1915 to defend the southern approaches to Istanbul; and the Sixth, Seventh, Eighth and Ninth Armies were set up during the course of the conflict.

The scale of mobilization was very large in proportion to the size of the Ottoman Empire's population. Losses, too, were high compared to other states – some 4,500,000 Turks alone dying during the conflict from war-action, disease, starvation and massacre. Even before entering the war there was a massive call-up of reserves which put a great strain on resources. The harvest was severely disrupted and this caused a near famine. Nevertheless several new Armies were established following massive troop movements across huge distances; the 6th Army Corps near Aleppo in Syria, for example, joining the First Army outside Istanbul.

Foreign observers were impressed by the quality of the First Army outside the capital although more distant Armies had lower efficiency with some infantry companies consisting of no more than 20 ill-equipped men. The First Army was based in the remnants of the Empire's European provinces (Eastern Thrace), the Second on the Asiatic side of the Bosphorus, not far from Istanbul, and the Third at Erzerum in eastern Turkey. By the end of the war nine numbered armies were in existence throughout the Empire, plus the special Yıldırım Army and several separate corps serving in Europe. The large number of these armies was criticized by German advisors who believed they required too many staff and support facilities which could have been better used at the front.

During the months of Ottoman neutrality Turkish war aims changed significantly, the westward ambitions being abandoned in favour of liberating of the Muslim-Turkish peoples of the Caucasus and Central Asia from Armenian and Russian domination. More immediately, Enver Paşa's first plan was a compromise between Ottoman and German priorities, with the pre-emptive strike against the Russian Black Sea fleet followed by defensive operations in the Caucasus and an offensive against the British-held Suez Canal while the bulk of the Army stood ready for possible action in the Ukraine.

Soon, the dream of liberating eastern Turkish peoples developed into an obsession. Enver drew up an extraordinary plan for a winter offensive against Russian forces in the Caucasus, a plan that Liman von Sanders considered impossible and which ended in disaster in January 1915. The defeat deprived the Ottomans of reserves of trained troops badly needed on other fronts. Such Pan-Turkish dreams diverted attention away from the Ottoman Empire's Arab provinces and eventually caused the Empire's undo-

Ottoman Turkish field artillery on the Gallipoli front in 1915. The loader's collar has the Arabic number 7 (a small V) indicating his regiment.

The rear-view of the kabalak of the man on the right shows how the cloth covering of this headgear was normally wound. (Askeri Müzesi, Istanbul)

ing. Only in the summer of 1917, with the proposed Yıdırım campaign, were these southern fronts taken seriously, but by then it was too late.

Morale

Amazingly, the morale of what even the most sympathetic modern military historian has called the *'rugged but gimcrack Ottoman Army'* remained high almost to the end. The dedication of Turkish units like the 57th Infantry Regiment, which was almost wiped out while stopping an Australian advance from ANZAC Cove during the Gallipoli campaign, is known, but not widely. What is less remembered is

Turkish officers captured by the 5th Australian Light Horse during the fall of Damascus, 30 September 1918. Most wear the lamb's fur kalpak but two cavalry officers have distinctive hats that look like deep-sea fishermen's 'sou'westers'. (Imperial War Museum Q12353)

Ottoman Army Organisation 1914–1918

Date	Location	Air Support	Comments
GHQ			
1914	Istanbul	Army-Navy Flying Schools	
1915	Istanbul	Army-Navy Flying Schools	
1916	Istanbul	Army-Navy Flying Schools, & 9th Sq. (formed Oct. for defence of Istanbul)	
1917	Istanbul	Army-Navy Flying Schools & 9th Sq.	
1918	Istanbul	Army-Navy Flying Schools & 9th Sq.	
First Army			
1914	Thrace		Formed 5 Aug. 1914
1915	Western shores of Straits		
1916	Thrace		
1917	Thrace	2nd Naval Sq. & German seaplane unit (as Straits Defence Command)	Two Corps sent to northern Syria; thereafter little more than 'name-plate'
1918	Thrace	2nd Naval Sq. & German seaplane unit (as Straits Defence Command)	Little more than 'name-plate' Disbanded 17 Feb. 1918 Reformed 24 Sept. 1918 Disbanded 11 Oct. 1918
Second Army			
1914	Thrace		Formed 5 Aug. 1914 Disbanded 18 Nov. 1914 Reformed 5 Dec. 1914
1915	Eastern shores of Straits		
1916	South-eastern Anatolia	10th Sq. (from Aug.)	Moved east Ap.–Aug. combined with 3rd Army as **Caucasus Army Group**
1917	South-eastern Anatolia, moved east after Russian Revolution	10th Sq.	Part of **Caucasus Army Group** (one Corps returned to Istanbul, rest of this Corps attached to **Sixth Army**)
1918	Caucasus & north-west Iran	7th Sq., 8th Sq., 10th Sq., 16th Sq., 3rd Naval Sq. & 17th Sq. (name-plate only)	Part of **Caucasus Army Group** (only seven battalions). Disbanded 15 Dec. 1918
Third Army			
1914	North-east Anatolia		Formed 5 Aug. 1914 1st Exped. Force sent to north-western Iran late 1914
1915	North-east Anatolia		5th Exped. Force sent to south-east Anatolia early 1915
1916	North-east Anatolia	7th Sq. & 8th Sq. (name-plate only)	Combined with **Second Army** as **Caucasus Army Group**
1917	Central & north-east Anatolia	7th Sq. & 8th Sq.	Part of **Caucasus Army Group**
1918	North-east Anatolia, to Georgia (Batum) & Azarbayjan (Baku)	(see under **Second Army**)	Part of **Caucasus Army Group** Irregular largely Azeri '**Islamic Army**' attached. Disbanded 15 Nov. 1918
	New **Third Army** being formed in Thrace. Staff only, 'name-plate'	15th Sq.	
Fourth Army			
1914	Syria, Palestine & Arabia (Hijaz & Yemen)		Formed 7 Sept. 1914 Suez Canal Exped. Formed late 1914
1915	Syria, Palestine & Arabia (Hijaz & Yemen)		Part of Canal Exped. Force to Gallipoli early 1915 Hijaz Exped.
1916	Cilicia, Syria, Palestine & Arabia	4th Sq., 3rd Sq. & 300th Paşa (German) Sq.	Southern part of Hijaz Exped. Force withdrawn into Madina May (remain to Jan. 1919), northern part in northern Hijaz & southern Jordan (until 1918). Seventh Corps (in Asir, Yemen & Aden) isolated from **Fourth Army** after Arab Revolt.
1917	Cilicia, Syria, Palestine & Arabia	Damascus Aircraft Park, 3rd Sq., 4th Sq., 14th Sq., 300th, 301st, 302nd, 303rd & 304th Paşa (German) Sqs.	Disbanded 26 Sept. 1917 Seventh Corps (in Asir, Yemen & Aden) isolated from **Fourth Army**

that a regiment of Arab reinforcements then drove the Australians back to the coast. Only later in the war did the morale of such non-Turkish units decline with the spread of the Arab Revolt. Victory in the Gallipoli campaign also boosted morale, this being the first time in living memory that an Ottoman Army had defeated a major European power.

As Mustafa Kemal Atatürk later wrote, the greatest monument to such successes was the *Mehmetçik* himself – the affectionate nickname given

Date	Location	Air Support	Comments
Fifth Army			
1915	Straits (Bosphorus & Dardanelles)	1st Sq. (from July)	Formed 25 Mar. 1915
1916	Straits (Bosphorus & Dardanelles), and western Anatolia	1st Sq., 6th Sq., 5th Sq. & 1st Naval Sq.	
1917	Western & south-western Anatolia, & Cilicia	1st Sq., 6th Sq., 5th Sq., 12th Sq. & 1st Naval Sq.	Only eight weak divisions
1918	Straits (Bosphorus & Dardanelles), and western Anatolia	1st Sq., 6th Sq., 5th Sq., 12th Sq., 1st Naval Sq., & 1st, 2nd, 3rd Balloon Sections	Disbanded 21 Nov. 1918
Sixth Army			
1915	Iraq		Formed 5 Sept. 1915 from units already in Iraq
1916	Iraq	2nd Sq. & 12th (later renamed 13th) Sq.	Mosul Group formed July to counter Russian threat to Mosul
1917	Central & northern Iraq	Baghdad Aircraft Park (moved to Samarra & later Mosul), 2nd Sq., 11th Sq., 13th Sq. & 1st Balloon Sq. (non-operational)	Separate Euphrates & Tigris Groups formed because of difficult communications
1918	Northern Iraq	Mosul Aircraft Park, 2nd & 13th Sq.	Still existed Jan. 1919
Seventh Army			
1917	Cilicia		Formed 12 Aug. 1917. Intended for Iraq front, diverted to Palestine
1918	Palestine & Syria	(see under **Yıldırım Army Group**)	Under **Yıldırım Army Group** command. Disbanded 13 Nov. 1918
Eighth Army			
1916	Palestine		Formed 2 Oct. 1916 (date uncertain)
1917	Palestine		
1918	Palestine & Syria	(see under **Yıldırım Army Group**)	Including **German Asia Corps** Under **Yıldırım Army Group** command. Disbanded 14 Nov. 1918)
Ninth Army			
1818	Balkans		Formed 9 June 1918 (name-plate only) incorporating Rumeli Field Detachment (see **European Fronts**) Still existed Jan. 1919
Yıldırım Army Group			
1917	Northern Syria & northern Iraq		Staff formed early 1917 (theoretically incorporating **Fourth, Seventh & Eighth Armies**, and **German Asia Corps**)
1918	Syria & Palestine	3rd Sq., 4th Sq., 14th Sq. & 300th, 301st, 302nd, 303rd, 304th, 305th (name-plate only) Paşa Sqs., and German Jasta 1F	Incorporating Amman Exped. Force (formed March incorporating Ma'an Exped. Force previously regarded as part of Hijaz Exped. Force)
European Fronts:			
Rumeli Field Detachment			177th Inf. Reg. only
1915	Thrace		Formed late 1915
1916	Western Macedonia		Sent to Bitola early 1916
1917	Western Macedonia		
1918	Western Macedonia		Incorporated into **Ninth Army** early 1918
6th Army Corps			Three Divisions
1916	Galicia		Under command of German Gen. Von Mackensen
1917	Galicia		
1918	Galicia		
15th Army Corps			Two Divisions
1916	Wallachia & Dobruja		
1917	Wallachia & Dobruja		
20th Army Corps			Two Divisions
1917	Eastern Macedonia		Attached to Bulgarian 2nd Army on Struma front
1918	Eastern Macedonia		

to the brave but unpretentious Turkish infantryman. The courage of *Mehmetçik* was recognized by allies and foes alike. In the Middle East, where the Arab peoples have little reason to be nostalgic about Ottoman rule, the Turkish soldier of the Great War is still remembered as *Abu Shuja'a*, the 'Father of Courage', while his British opponent is remembered as *Abu Alf Midfah*, the 'Father of a Thousand Guns'. On the other hand most observers recognized that the uneducated Ottoman ordinary soldier was lost without good leadership and that any breakdown of command weakened his morale. At Gallipoli leaders like Mustafa Kemal understood the capabilities of such troops when well commanded by officers who led by personal example. There were many examples of silent pre-dawn attacks in which officers with drawn swords went ahead of men who were ordered to charge only when they saw their officers raise their whips and only to shout their battle-cry of *Allahu Akbar* when they had actually reached the enemy's trenches. The close relationship between officers and men was, however, gradually undermined. By the end of 1917 a frequent reshuffling of Armies, the breaking up and re-forming of units, meant that officers hardly knew their men, let alone had time to earn their respect.

Not surprisingly Arab units were the first to show signs of decay. Turkish (essentially anti-Arab) nationalism grew quickly within the Ottoman Army and had undermined the morale of many Arab officers even before the war began. According to Liman von Sanders the Arab was just as good a soldier as the Turk – when treated fairly – but by 1917 this was no longer the case. By 1918 most Arab troops were held back as an unreliable reserve.

Islam

Competing nationalisms may have influenced the Ottoman Army's officer corps but it was the Muslim faith which underpinned the morale of the ordinary Ottoman soldier. It also had a powerful influence on some senior commanders. Fahri Paşa, the Ottoman Commander in the Muslim Holy City of Medina for example, had been cut off from support for years and only surrendered in 1919 after receiving specific orders from the Ottoman sultan. He then left his sword on the Prophet Muhammad's grave and retired as a hero to Turkish Muslims. Throughout the Ottoman Army Muslim *imams* served much as Christian chaplains did in European armies. They are recorded reading the Qur'an to soldiers as they served their guns under naval bombardment at Gallipoli and later reportedly took over the leadership of some

Above: Turkish anti-aircraft gun camouflaged to look like a small bush. The officers in front include both Turks and Germans. (Cross & Cockade International)

Gunners with a 105 mm howitzer, in action 1918. The gun was a standard German field piece. White uniforms were often worn by artillerymen in hot weather, but less usual are the men's sandals. Once again their officer wears a quite distinctive uniform. (Imperial War Museum Q52142)

infantry platoons after all the officers had been killed. The Bektasi dervish organization had a particularly close connection with the Ottoman Army that went right back to the founding of the state. Supposedly suppressed in 1826, it had enjoyed a revival in the early 20th century and during the Great War played its traditional religious role, supporting the men's morale. Being regarded by Europeans as the most reformist of such dervish 'sects', the Bektasi went on to support Mustafa Kemal's Turkish Nationalists against the Ottoman Sultan after the war. Volunteer military units were also recruited from other dervish sects such as the Mevlevi (Whirling Dervishes) and the Qadariya (Fatalist) orders.

Morale was one thing, standards of training quite another, and it was clear that these varied between Armies in different parts of the Empire. In Gallipoli Ottoman marksmanship, particularly that of sharpshooters, was generally superior to that of the invaders. Standards declined considerably towards the end of the war but even as late as April and May 1918, in what is now Jordan, pony-mounted Turkish cavalry succeeded in driving back larger numbers of superbly mounted troopers from the Australian Mounted Division.

To compound these problems, the lure of eastward expansion led to some extraordinary schemes in the War Ministry back in Istanbul. One of Enver Paşa's more fanciful plans was to send three regiments through neutral Iran to stir up an anti-British revolt in India. In 1917, as British pressure mounted in both Iraq and Palestine, Turkish officers were still being offered promotion and increased pay if they volunteered for service on the Caucasus front. Even as late as 1918, in the very closing stages of the war, Turkish troops and senior officers were still being withdrawn from Syria to reinforce a thrust through the Caucasus. Meanwhile entire battalions of unwilling Arab conscripts were deserting before they even reached the fronts. The Ottoman High Command's decision to send many of its best units to various European fronts was, however, a purely political decision to show solidarity with Germany, Austria-Hungary and Bulgaria. Liman von Sanders considered it correct to send such troops against Romania, which could have threatened Ottoman Thrace, but a mistake to send others to Galicia or to the Bulgarian front in northern Greece.

Desertion

By 1918 desertion had become a serious problem. At the beginning of the war many Armenian soldiers deserted to the Russians, and then re-enlisted as fanatically anti-Turkish volunteers. As a result most of the remaining Armenian troops in the Ottoman Army were disarmed and converted into poorly fed,

Machine gunners in action, Palestine front. The officers have grey collars on their tunics while the men's uniforms carry no distinguishing marks. (Imperial War Museum Q56641)

Section from a mounted machine-gun detachment in action at Beersheba. Such units again reflected the more mobile character of the Great War in the Middle East. (Copyright Westminster Dragoons Museum Trust; photograph supplied by the National Army Museum, London)

harshly treated labour battalions. Troops of Arab origin were the next to start deserting in some numbers, but by late 1917 when rations on the Caucasus, Syrian and Iraqi fronts had deteriorated to almost below subsistence level, even Turks were doing so. Frequent amnesties were announced from the Sultan's palace in attempts to bring troops back to the ranks, much to the disgust of German advisors who argued in favour of salutary executions to discourage further desertion.

Even in 1914 some Ottoman Armies had not been up to full strength and as the war dragged on several of those in quiet areas were reduced to little more than 'number-plates'. The Fifth Army in western Anatolia had, after the end of the Gallipoli campaign, only about one-third of its proper artillery, virtually no transport, and almost no machine-guns; some of its troops even lacked rifles. By 1917 most military formations were only at one-fifth paper strength, and even the best units were losing half their new recruits through desertion or sickness before they reached their regiments. Most of the remaining troops were raw recruits conscripted as young as 16 years of age. In isolated locations such as the scattered garrisons defending the Hijaz railways, however, numbers were actually above the official strengths as 'unlisted', unpaid stragglers were attracted by the chance of food.

The morale of the civilian population, particularly in Istanbul, endured remarkably well. Every student of modern Turkish history knows how Mustafa Kemal Atatürk forced 'modernization' and 'Westernization' on his people after the First World War. Yet the war itself had already seen considerable liberalization. These were most obvious in the role of women and, unlike some ideas subsequently forced on the people by Atatürk, this earlier relaxation generally remained within Islamic codes of behaviour. During the war, for example, many Turkish women in Istanbul discarded the veil in public – to the horror of ultra-traditionalists. Yet they almost invariably retained the headscarf, this being all that the Prophet Muhammad had originally insisted upon. More importantly, Ottoman women played a prominent role in offices, factories, relief and medical work just as women did in other countries caught up in the Great War.

UNIFORMS AND EQUIPMENT

One of the most visible results of the Young Turk Revolution of 1908–9 was in Ottoman Army uniforms, although these reforms took several years to complete. During the previous hundred years the Ottoman Empire had often tried to modernize the appearance as well as the organization of its armed forces. At the time of the Crimean War there had been a strong French influence but by the late 19th century the Army was modelling itself almost entirely upon German fashions.

A basic khaki uniform was introduced in 1909 to replace the old dark blue, although these remained for an officer's full-dress uniform. The red *tarbush* or 'fez' with its dark blue tassel, the trademark of the Turkish soldier for almost a century, was replaced by the *kabalak*. This unique form of military headgear consisted of a long cloth wound around a wickerwork base and resembling a solar topee or sun-helmet. The *kabalak* had apparently been devised by Enver Paşa himself and was often known as an *Enveriye*. Officers wore the sheepskin *kalpak* but this was normally replaced by a *kabalak* on active service. Later in the war a simplified form of *kabalak* was introduced for officers, with a plain khaki covering and a single strip of cloth wound once around the helmet. Troops of Arab origin generally wore their traditional *kufiya* headcloths.

The quality of uniforms worn by officers and other ranks seems to have differed even more in the Ottoman Army than elsewhere. Many officers, particularly those of senior rank, had their dress as well as their personal weapons made in Germany. Some ordinary soldiers' kit was also manufactured by the Ottoman Empire's central European allies but the bulk of uniforms seem to have been made in Turkey itself. Towards the end of the war the quality of these ranged from moderately good to simply appalling. Colours as well as quality of cloth varied considerably. The same applied to boots and other leather items.

On campaign equipment could often not be replaced so that soldiers were seen with their feet bound in cloth and their worn leather equipment held together with string. During the appalling weather of November 1915 Ottoman troops at Gallipoli were also supplied with a strange assortment of warm clothing donated by the people of Istanbul, including unsuitably fashionable underwear and gentlemen's lightweight shoes. Footwear was to become a real problem for the Ottoman Army and by the summer of 1917 even some officers had not got proper boots.

On the other hand certain details of insignia had a

A unit of mevlavi *dervish volunteers in Istanbul, 1915. They are led by drummers and are distinguished by a special form of flat-topped cap with a small turban wound around it. One of the men standing guard also carries a long double-bladed axe, a weapon associated with the Ottoman Empire's famous Janissary infantry and still used as a mark of rank by dervish volunteer units during World War One. (Askeri Müzesi, Istanbul)*

The Caucasus front in 1917. A staff officer is photographed with a ten-year-old boy soldier who has his slain father's rifle and his medal. (Askeri Müzesi, Istanbul)

cated by the number of pips and the degree of braiding on shoulder-boards; NCO ranks by simple stripes around the sleeve.

At about the same time as the simpler form of officer's *kabalak* was being introduced for the Army, the Ottoman Navy brought in new headgear reflecting German influence. This was essentially a normal European naval cap, but it lacked a peak in deference to Islamic tradition, so that a man might touch his forehead to the ground while making his *salat* or ritual prayer without removing his hat. This was an extremely important consideration: only a few years later Turkey's fanatically secular new leader, Kemal Atatürk, insisted that men wear European peaked 'flat caps' as a direct challenge to Islamic tradition – a large number of people were killed in the ensuing riots.

long pedigree and can still be seen in the Turkish Army of today. Branches of service were indicated by coloured collars for officers, collar patches for other ranks, repeated in the edging of officers' *kalabak* covering: infantry – olive green, machine-gun companies – grass green, cavalry – light grey, artillery – dark blue, engineers – mid-blue, railway troops – sky blue, gendarmerie – scarlet. In 1915 the Ottoman Air Service was separated from the Engineers and changed from blue collar patches to red. Officer and warrant-officer ranks were, as in most armies, indi-

Logistics

The Ottoman Empire was ill-prepared for a prolonged war effort, with almost no munitions industries of its own. Huge armies and their material would have to be moved along earth roads, tracks and incomplete single-line railways over vast distances through exceptionally difficult terrain and extreme climatic conditions. The Ottoman Armies remained heavily dependent on supplies from their German and Austro-Hungarian allies throughout the war.

Stockpiles of munitions had largely been used up during the Balkan Wars; in 1914 the most pressing shortages were of artillery shells and naval mines. Within a few days of signing the secret treaty with Germany, Enver Paşa told his new allies that he needed 500,000 shells and 200,000 rifles. Late August and early September saw further requests for 200 mines, then howitzers, trucks, electrical equipment, tools, uniforms, boots, blankets and canned food. Only a fraction of this *materiél* arrived before the Ottoman Empire entered the war, whereupon shipments through neutral Bulgaria and Romania became almost impossible. Once Bulgaria joined the German alliance, followed by the conquest of Serbia and Romania however, the shipment of supplies became

Turkish reservists being called to the colours in Anatolia, March 1917. The Ottoman Army was able to provide its reservists with reasonable equipment almost to the end of the Great War. (Imperial War Museum, Q60323)

easier. Germany, and to a lesser extent Austria-Hungary, began sending vitally needed guns, ammunition, communications equipment, aircraft and other high-technology items. They also had to supply coal after the Russian fleet disrupted seaborne supplies from the Ottoman Empire's own mines in northern Anatolia.

During the course of the war, German experts tried to improve the chaotic Ottoman logistical system, but with little success: most Ottoman Armies had to live off the land much as they had done for centuries. The Ottoman Army was not, of course, entirely dependent on outside help. Though even traditional craftsmen had largely been ruined by cheap foreign imports, a number of government factories had been established for basic military items such as uniforms and packs. More technical production facilities also appeared during the war, a German naval captain named Pieper Paşa helping set up munitions factories while Austro-Hungarian technicians supervised a new propeller-making workshop.

Of more immediate concern was the effect that massive mobilization had on food production, with famine as the inevitable result. During the war, supplies of draft horses also slumped to 40 per cent, oxen and buffaloes to 15 per cent. The shortage of draft animals, and disease among the remainder (the country only had 250 vets), was a serious problem for the Ottoman Army which had constantly to requisition more from the peasants – disrupting agriculture even further. Even when beasts of burden were available they were not always suitable for the conditions in which the Ottoman Armies fought. In eastern Anatolia during winter, animals could not get through the snowbound mountains and ammunition had to be brought to the front on the shoulders of peasant women volunteers.

Small arms

The personal equipment of the Ottoman soldier was essentially German in design, though reduced to the barest essentials, while weapons were almost all of German manufacture. Officers were armed with swords, though these were not generally carried in action, and they generally purchased their own pistols of European commercial design. The infantry rifle was the Turkish Mauser, of either Model 1893 or Model 1903 (for short 'M.1893' or 'M.1903'). Later supplies included German M.1888 rifles, the so-called Commission Rifle, and apparently some German Mauser M.1898s while the Austrians sent adapted Russian Mossin-Nagant M.1891 rifles. Some reservists may even have carried the obsolete black-powder Turkish Mauser M.1887. Bayonets were made by a number of German companies in Solingen and Suhl. Some Ottoman infantry also seem to have carried fighting knives in their boots, just as their medieval predecessors had done. Cavalry were armed with a rifle or carbine, the latter usually being the Turkish Mauser M.1905. They also carried a sword or lance or both, the sword being either the M.1909 made by Carl Eickhorn of Solingen or an earlier model. The supply situation could be very

Colours of an unknown regiment and its colour guard during a medal-giving ceremony on the Palestine front. The ribbons hanging from the flagstaff represent medals given to this unit as a whole. (Askeri Müzesi, Istanbul)

different on each of the fronts, particularly in the latter part of the war when one unit of 8,000 men was recorded as only having 1,000 rifles.

Artillery and other weapons

Despite severe losses during the Balkan Wars, the Ottoman Army still possessed German, British, French and other artillery in 1914. During the course of the war new guns came from German or Austro-Hungarian manufacturers. Krupp was the most important supplier, though at first demanded immediate cash payment.

The almost complete lack of heavy guns was the Ottoman Army's greatest problem. During the Anglo-French naval bombardment of the Dardanelles dummy batteries were set up; these were allegedly manned by two old reservists each armed with a length of stove-pipe and several smoke cartridges which they lit at random intervals before scampering back into shallow dugouts. During the Gallipoli campaign the Ottomans pressed into service century-old mortars from the Army Museum in Istanbul. Fortunately the collapse of Serbia opened up a direct supply route, allowing several big howitzers to arrive from Austria, along with a quantity of mountain artillery. Nevertheless Ottoman Armies on the Caucasus front were always chronically short of artillery.

There was always a dearth of machine-guns, the Ottomans only having a handful of Maxims and Hotchkiss at the start of the war. As far as other weapons were concerned, the Ottoman Navy's mines included Russian examples retrieved from the sea outside Trabzon, French from off Izmir, and even old Bulgarian mines from the previous Balkan wars. A lack of land-mines meant that torpedo-heads were used in the shore defences of the Dardanelles while ordinary garden wire from nearby farms was

Left: A Turkish heavy artillery battery at Gallipoli in 1915. These large guns fought off the first Allied attempt to force a way through the Straits by naval power alone. The man in the background wears the white shirt with bands of grouped narrow black stitching often worn beneath a soldier's tunic. (Askeri Müzesi, Istanbul)

An ox-drawn heavy gun on the march, 1917, probably an Austro-Hungarian-made Skoda 149mm howitzer. Several onlookers appear to wear Austro-Hungarian uniforms and the buildings in the background suggest that this photograph was taken on the Galician front. It certainly illustrates the logistical difficulties faced by the Turks in mountainous terrain lacking proper roads. (Imperial War Museum Q60340)

stretched underwater near vulnerable beaches. Ottoman forces were similarly short of sandbags, many of these being used by the soldiers to patch their tattered uniforms. So short were the soldiers of entrenching tools that they captured these from the enemy whenever possible. Their officers, meanwhile, found that maps they captured from the British were superior to the *Baedeker* 'tourist guides' on which they had often had to rely.

GERMAN INFLUENCE

Since most European and American historians base their work on German rather than untranslated Turkish sources, there has been widespread exaggeration of the role of the Germans in the Ottoman war effort. There were, in fact, around 500 German officers in the Ottoman Empire when war broke out and some were immediately put in command of Ministry of War departments including Operations, Intelligence, Railways, Supply, Munitions, Coal and Fortresses. Once direct overland communications with Germany were opened a great many more German officers and NCOs were sent to serve in the Ottoman Army, Navy and Air Forces. Towards the end of the war relatively large German combat units also arrived, most importantly in Palestine.

In the autumn of 1917, however, the relationship changed. The German military mission was replaced by a German-Ottoman military convention. Under this new arrangement many Turkish officers were sent to Germany for advanced training while there was less direct German supervision of basic Ottoman Army training. Ottoman divisions were reconstructed along German lines, though it remains unclear how far these changes were carried through in practice. The Germans complained about what they saw as an unnecessary volume of Ottoman paperwork, though the records show that Turkish and Arab officers were also often less than impressed by their German colleagues. The Germans, with few exceptions, failed to understand the Turkish mentality or to show sensitivity to the Ottoman Empire's proud Islamic heritage, often making it all too obvious that they saw themselves as superior to both Turks and Arabs. On the Ottoman side young officers, particularly those who favoured the new Turkish nationalism, resented being treated as second-class soldiers.

In terms of broad war aims the Ottoman and German High Commands had been at odds since the war began. After the Russian Revolution the Turks found themselves facing even greater opposition from Germany than from Russia in attempts to regain eastern territory. In the meantime Germans, British and Turks all had their eyes on the Baku oil fields of Azarbayjan.

German officer inspecting a company of Turkish storm-troopers in Palestine, probably in 1918. The soldiers and their commander wear the special Turkish steel helmet which differed slightly from that of German troops. (Imperial War Museum Q80044)

TRANSPORT

The very inadequacy of the Ottoman Empire's communications gave them a special significance during the First World War.

Rail

The only proper modern railway service was in the Balkans, but most of this had been lost in 1913. The railways system in the Asian provinces was very limited, single track and fragmented. Within Anatolia some incomplete lines were linked by narrow-gauge track while a third gauge was used in Lebanon, sixty soldiers being allocated to every freight car for the frequent transloading. The stations were tiny and could not cope with large volumes of military traffic while the limited rolling stock meant that only a hundred small trains could be made up. Even Major Kübel, the German military transport expert attached to the Ottoman railway service, criticized the German-controlled Anatolian and Baghdad Railway Company for not providing the services that the Ottoman Army was entitled to, criticism repeated by his successor Lt. Col. Böttrich. The fact that most railway technicians were militarily unreliable non-Turks merely compounded such problems. Then there was the question of fuel. South of the Taurus mountains locomotives used wood instead of coal. This required over 31,000 soldiers and devastated the forests of surrounding provinces. By 1917 engines were fuelled with cotton seed, liquorice, olive branches, vines and even camel dung! South of the Taurus the single-track railway also ran close to the Gulf of Iskenderun where it was vulnerable to naval gunfire. This area was also a nodal point in the entire system and as such the Ottoman Army had to be on guard against possible Allied landings. Constant attacks on the railway lines through Syria, Jordan and Arabia by the Hashemite Arab Army not only interrupted schedules but were increasingly difficult to repair due to a shortage of materials.

Road

Military historians have given less attention to the Ottoman road system which was even weaker than the rail network. The Empire was actually in the process of a large road-building scheme in 1914, though the projects so far completed were all in western provinces and so only influenced the Gallipoli campaign. The first eight months of the war saw a huge repair and road-building effort by military labour battalions, continuing until February 1916 in Syria, Jordan and Palestine where sections of the resulting well-paved roads are still visible. The role of animal power can hardly be exaggerated and the Ottoman Army's efforts in the Great War have been described as a losing battle between the Turkish

A Turkish military policeman with the crew of the captured British submarine E15 which ran aground in the Dardanelles on 17 April 1915. These men wore standard infantry uniforms plus a large brass gorget inscribed with the word Kanun, meaning 'Law', and yellow aiguillette cords on the right breast.

Senior officers & ceremonial dress
1: Mustafa Kemal Bey, General Staff service dress, 1915
2: Enver Paşa, dress uniform c.1917
3: Standard bearer with regimental flag, Nişancı (Rifle) Battalion

Infantry
1: Turkish line infantryman, marching order, c.1914
2: Infantryman, off duty, Galicia c.1917
3: Arab bicycle infantry, Arabia 1915

Cavalry
1: Cavalry officer
2: NCO of a Turkish cavalry regiment, c.1917
3: Kurdish irregular officer

C

Specialist Troops
1: Assault party, 1918
2: Ski-troops NCO, Caucasus c.1917
3: Officer, machine-gun detachment

Artillery
1: Artillery officer, Gallipoli 1915
2: Artillery officer, Galicia
3: Artillery Sergeant, Galicia

Air Forces
1: Naval Pilot Engineer Mülazim (Lieutenant) Ahmet of the Naval Flying School, Yesilköy, dress uniform
2: Army Air Force Observer Mülazim (Lieutenant) Sitki, No. 4 Squadron, southern Anatolia 1917
3: German volunteer Pilot Kleinehayk of No. 10 Squadron, southern Anatolia, summer 1917

F

Navy
1: Sailor of naval landing party, Palestine
2: Able seaman
3: Commander, winter uniform 1915

kagni or ox-cart and the enemy's railways, steamships and motor lorries. On the Caucasus front even the rugged *kagni* could not be used and here Ottoman troops were often supplied by caravans of pack animals. Add to this a lack of maps for many areas, the destruction of bridges by winter weather, snow in the mountains from September to May, a nearest railhead over six hundred miles away, and it seems hardly surprising that munitions took six weeks to reach the Caucasus. Eventually German engineers built a motor road as far as Sivas but the Ottoman Army had no motor transport, other than a few staff cars, and so could provide no technical support for trucks when these arrived. Even in the relatively kind conditions of Gallipoli teams of buffaloes hauled the heavy artillery and if hills got in the way hundreds of soldiers pulled these guns with ropes.

Sea

Before the war, maritime communications had been vital for the Ottoman Empire. Once war broke out the Red Sea, eastern Mediterranean and Aegean were closed by the overwhelming power of enemy navies. The Turks and their Yemeni sympathizers could use small dhows along the Red Sea coast and such vessels even maintained contact with Ottoman allies in Somalia and Eritrea. Smugglers continued to ply the Mediterranean and Aegean coasts of Anatolia despite British, French and Italian patrols. From the summer of 1915 until the Revolution of 1917 the Russian fleet prevented large Ottoman ships from sailing the Black Sea, and strangled vital shipments of coal from Zonguldak to Istanbul. Small amounts were still moved in sailing ships, the Russians claiming to have sunk about a thousand of these during the war. The Black Sea was opened once more after the Russian Revolution but before then the Ottoman state ran short of coal, much of which had to be brought by rail from central Europe. Even the almost enclosed Sea of Marmara was made hazardous by enemy submarines, supported as they were by Greek sympathizers living on the coast, although Liman von Sanders considered the effectiveness of the submarine war to have been exaggerated by British naval historians.

The Ottoman Empire also had a remarkably effective telegraph service operating over huge distances but the country had no wireless before the war, nor were there any telephones outside Istanbul. The Ottoman Sultan could telephone the Kaiser in Berlin but, frustratingly, not his own commanders at the front.

THE NAVY

The Ottoman Navy played only a minor role in the First World War for the simple reason that it was not designed to face the British and French fleets. Considerable effort had been put into strengthening the Navy between 1909 and 1914 but the foes envisaged at that time were Greeks and possibly Russians. A British Rear Admiral also supervised a major naval reorganization. In fact British Royal Navy influence was so strong that, from 1910, not only were Ottoman ships painted the same colours as those of Britain but officer insignia also mirrored those of the Royal Navy. Turkish technical officers had the same colours between their sleeve ranking

Ottoman troops crossing the Tigris or Euphrates in a gufa, *a type of primitive bitumen-covered reed boat that had been used in Iraq for thousands of years. One man wears the Arab head* kufiya *cloth while the others have the old-fashioned soft* fezes *still worn by Turkish troops when off duty.*

stripes as did the British. Orders were placed in Britain and France for new vessels ranging from battleships to gunboats; and the Ottoman yards at Samsun, Izmir, Beirut and Basra competed to see who could make the best small ships in the shortest time. The Navy was a popular arm of service, the exploits of the ex-American cruiser *Hamidiye* under Hüseyin Rauf in the Aegean and Adriatic having been a great boost to public morale during the otherwise catastrophic First Balkan War.

During the months of Ottoman neutrality the Fleet steered well clear of action. In the meantime the influence of the British naval advisory mission collapsed, and its personnel were replaced by Germans. The main arsenal was in Istanbul and, with around 6,000 personnel, the Navy's primary role was to survive as a threat to any enemy attacking the capital. It also had to protect supply convoys in the Sea of Marmara and, as far as possible, the Black Sea.

By the outbreak of war the Ottoman Navy consisted of three archaic pre-dreadnought battleships, *Hayruddin Barbarossa* (1893), *Turgut Reis* (1894) and *Mesudiye* (1874), to which were added the German battlecruiser *Goeben* renamed as the *Sultan Selim Yavuz* (1912) and the light cruiser *Breslau* now called *Midilli* (1912). In support was the even older coastal defence pre-dreadnought battleship *Muin-i-Zafer* (1869) and the slightly more modern light cruisers *Hamidiye* (1903) and *Mecidiye* (1903). The Ottoman Navy also had eight destroyers, seven torpedo-boats, three torpedo-gunboats, perhaps nine other gunboats, an old gunboat converted for minelaying and approximately eleven lightly armed motor launches. Support vessels included a torpedo depot ship, a hospital ship, four troop transports and a naval transport, a naval repair vessel, three smaller despatch vessels, and an Imperial yacht. During or immediately prior to the war a minelayer was added to this fleet. Construction of six small German-designed destroyers was believed to have been started in Istanbul during the war and although none are said to have been completed, the Ottoman Navy did end the war with an extra destroyer in addition to surviving pre-war vessels. It also ended up with an extra torpedo-boat. There are also reports that attempts were made during the war to refit two derelict German submarines, though without much success.

In the face of overwhelmingly more numerous enemies, the Ottoman Navy attempted few offensive operations, although HMS *Goliath* was sunk by the Ottoman torpedo boat *Muavenet Milli* under Commander Ahmet Efendi on 13 May 1915. The navy's

Above: Petty-officers of the Ottoman Naval Air Service. These men were undergoing technical training at the Yesilköy flying school near Istanbul in 1917. (Havacılık Müzesi, Istanbul)

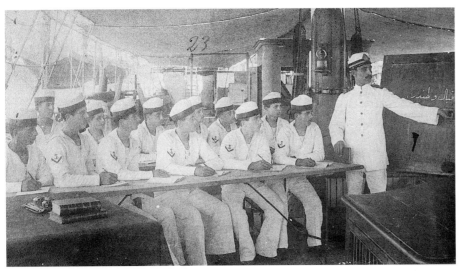

Midshipmen in their white summer uniforms under instruction by an officer on board a Turkish gunboat. The officer also wears his summer service uniform with the typical Ottoman peakless cap. (Deniz Müzesi, Istanbul)

Turkish Navy officials inspect the captured British submarine *E15* which ran aground in April 1915. The officer on the right with a note-pad is a sub-lieutenant from a technical branch and has no 'curl' on his single sleeve ring. In the distance on the left is a commander with three rings and 'curl'. Next to him stand several sailors in their dark blue winter uniforms.

main role was convoy protection, particularly in the Sea of Marmara. The second British submarine to enter this area, *E 15*, was sunk by the Ottomans, followed by the Australian *AE 2* which was also destroyed by a torpedo-boat. The *E 14* next got into the Marmara, where it sunk the transport ship *Gül Cemal*, though during a later attempt to penetrate the Dardanelles in 1918 the *E 14* was itself destroyed by an Ottoman vessel. Torpedo boats were particularly important, escorting convoys which stuck close inshore so that the Navy only had to protect one flank.

The Ottoman Navy's own most serious losses were during coastal protection duties. The old battleship *Mesudiye* was torpedoed by submarine *B 11* in the Dardanelles on 13 December 1914, the *Hayruddin Barbarossa* by *E 11* in the Sea of Marmara on 8 August 1915, though the *Turgut Reis* survived. All three of these were used as floating batteries during the Gallipoli campaign. The Ottoman Navy and Army combined in various small offensives against Aegean islands. Here captured documents suggested that Greek pirates were directed by Allied intelligence to raid the Turkish mainland for booty and to carry off women, children and cattle. Despite a lack of proper minelaying vessels the Ottoman Navy laid at least 423 mines during the war, more than France and nearly as many as Italy. Isolated from the rest of the Ottoman Fleet several river gunboats operated in Iraq, two being captured by the British.

By the end of the war the Ottoman Navy had lost, in addition to the two old pre-dreadnought battleships, the new German light cruiser *Midilli/Breslau* mined off Imbros in 1918. The smaller protected cruiser *Mecidiye* had been sunk by a mine in the Black Sea in 1915, raised and repaired by the Russian Navy only to be retaken by the Ottomans in 1918. Two torpedo gunboats claimed sunk by the British in 1915, the *Peyk-i-Sevket* torpedoed by *E2* and the *Burç-i Satvet* torpedoed by *E14*, had in fact been beached and repaired. Another torpedo gunboat had, however, been sunk while at least three ordinary gunboats were lost along with three destroyers and three torpedo boats.

THE AIR FORCES

In 1914 the Ottoman air arm was founded under the guidance of a French officer, Captain De Goys. During the war he was quickly replaced by a German, Major Erich Sarno. When the Ottomans entered the war they had six landplanes, four of which were operational; in addition to four ground instruction aircraft, two seaplanes and an observation balloon. There were only ten qualified pilots, who were supported by a small number of mechanics of whom many were Armenians of doubtful loyalty.

Even before hostilities broke out one Nieuport seaplane was sent to support the Dardanelles defences, and another soon followed. Two Bleriots were intended for the Caucasus Front but instead patrolled the northern entrance to the Bosphorus. A newly arrived and relatively modern Rumpler biplane was, meanwhile, sent to Syria. The Ottoman's first operational flight of the Great War was probably a seaplane reconnaissance off the Dardanelles on 17 August 1914 – shortly before the Empire actually entered the conflict. This Nieuport seaplane was replaced by a Bleriot on 5 November, and this solitary monoplane nick-named *Ertugrul*, made several flights over the British and French fleets during the build-up to the Gallipoli campaign. The first Ottoman

Aircrew under training at the Ottoman Air Forces training school, Yesilköy, probably in 1917. The Ottoman personnel included Army and Naval officers but this group also includes two Iranians, Ahmet Han standing on the left and Hussain Han behind him to the left. Both went on to fly as observers in the Ottoman Air Force's No. 14 Squadron based at Amman in present-day Jordan. (Havacılık Müzesi, Istanbul)

A group of pilots, trainees and instructors in front of one of the Ottoman Air Force's few Bleriot XI-2 monoplanes at the Yesilköy flying school near Istanbul. Pilot First Lt. Cemal Durusoy, seated on the port wing of this aircraft (nicknamed Ertugrul), flew several hazardous reconnaissance missions over the British fleet as it bombarded the Dardanelles forts in March 1915. In Turkey Cemal Durusoy and the Naval Lieutenant, Hüseyin Sedat, are regarded as the two most important flying heroes of the Gallipoli campaign. (Havacılık Müzesi, Istanbul)

victory in air combat came on 30 November 1915 when Lt. Ali Riza and Lt. Orhan in an Albatros CI shot down a French Farman near the Dardanelles. Deliveries of new German aircraft started by air in March 1915 and, in addition to the five German aircraft sold before the war, Germany went on to supply over 260 aircraft though not all had arrived safely or entered service before the war ended. The Ottoman Air Force also added 12 aircraft captured from the Russians and British, several of which were flown against their original owners.

The first numbered Ottoman Air Force squadron was formed at Galata and Çanakkale in January 1915, and as the war continued many more were

Pilot Lt. Orhan of the Ottoman Air Service's No. 3 Squadron with his Pfalz A II monoplane in 1916. Following the sudden Arab Revolt, this squadron was hurriedly transferred from the Caucasus to the Hijaz where it was thrown into battle against Lawrence and his Arab guerrilla forces. Lt. Orhan wears normal service uniform, with Air Force wings on his kalpak. (Havacılık Müzesi, Istanbul)

created. In 1917 Ottoman squadrons varied from a single aircraft with two pilots and two observers to 22 aircraft with 13 pilots and 13 observers. By the end of the war there were 18 squadrons in existence, varying in strength from a single pilot and no observer, to 12 pilots and 18 observers. The Ottoman Air Force operated from 66 airfields during the war, seven of them in occupied neutral or enemy territory (four in Iran, one in Egyptian Sinai and two in what had been the Russian Empire). Although German personnel played a vital role in development, technical support and operations, this should not be exaggerated. Most, though not all, fighter pilots were German; but men of Turkish, Arab and even Iranian origin dominated the observation squadrons. By the end of the war, following determined efforts to train Ottoman personnel, all three Naval squadrons as well as five Army squadrons were commanded by Ottoman officers; four squadrons were under joint command, and only six remained under German officers.

AUXILIARIES AND ALLIES

(*Note*: Some of these groups were covered in MAA 208: *Lawrence and the Arab Revolt*, including pro-Ottoman Arab tribes in Arabia and Yemen, the Sanussi in Libya, the Tuareg, various Saharan peoples and the 'Ali Dinar revolt in Darfur.)

European concepts of nationalism had been felt in the Ottoman Empire for at least a century; first among the Greeks, then Serbs and Bulgarians, then amongst Armenians, Macedonians and even the Turks themselves, and finally the Arabs. Wars of 'national liberation', massacres and counter-massacres had characterized Ottoman history throughout the 19th century and extreme nationalists were indulging in horrific acts of violence – guerrilla resistance to their supporters, terrorism to the Ottoman authorities. In 1909 the 'Young Turk' government banned the carrying of arms in mixed Slav, Greek and Albanian Macedonia and in the partially Armenian eastern provinces of Anatolia while the Army set up special anti-terrorist 'pursuit battalions'.

Within what remained of the Ottoman Empire in

A patrol of Turkish ski soldiers in the Caucasus. Such mountain troops were essential in a mountainous region which was snowbound for many months. Each man uses only a single ski-pole. (Askeri Müzesi, Istanbul)

1914 there were many competing nationalisms, some highly developed, others only stirring. The Arabs, for example, were the second most numerous people after the Turks, and although Arab nationalism had existed among the educated urban elite for generations, it only took root among ordinary people in reaction to the Turkish nationalism of the Young Turk government. During the early part of the Great War the authorities tried to Turkify the Arabs of Syria, but this proved to be impossible and by 1918 some Turk nationalists were even advocating Arab independence within a new federated state – too late of course.

There were many Turkish-speaking Orthodox Christians in Anatolia, some of whom identified themselves with the Greeks. They tended to keep a low profile, however, and were little affected by the war. The Jews of the Ottoman Empire were generally very loyal, those from long-established *Shephardi* communities outside Palestine (where the status of the recent Zionist colonizers was more sensitive) often enjoying a prosperous position in a state with no tradition of anti-semitism.

Armenians

Armenians, however, were in a very different situation. Unbiased estimates number the Armenian population of the Ottoman Empire at almost 1,250,000. But these Armenian Christians were themselves divided amongst Orthodox, Catholic and Protestant groups. They were also very scattered and nowhere formed a majority except in a tiny corner of eastern Anatolia. Elsewhere in Anatolia they comprised 15 to 25 per cent of the population. The details of the Armenian massacres that took place during the First World War are hotly disputed by historians with differing sympathies. All, however, tend to agree that they resulted from the 19th century spread of the European concept of nationalism in an area previously noted for centuries of relative harmony between linguistic, cultural and religious groups. It is also clear that all sides were guilty of the most appalling barbarity during the Great War, some carried out with the full knowledge of a political or military leadership, other resulting from banditry or from uncaring incompetence on the part of local authorities.

When the Great War broke out, it was immediately apparent that most Armenians both inside and outside Ottoman territory sympathized with the Allied cause. In August 1914 the senior Armenian religious leader resident in Russian-ruled territory proclaimed it a sacred duty for all Armenians to support the Russians. Inevitably most Armenian soldiers in the Ottoman Army were disarmed and sent to work in labour battalions. Armenian revolutionary cells already existed but there is disagreement about how far they fought in support of Russia. Armenian volunteers certainly started killing Muslim civilians as soon as Russian troops crossed the Ottoman frontier. At the same time large numbers of Armenian deserters from the Ottoman Army were enlisted as allies and auxiliary forces by the Russians. The rest of this sad story is one of massacre and counter-massacre by and upon Kurds, Armenians, Turks, Christian and Muslim Georgians, as well as the uprooting and deportation of entire populations by both Ottoman and Russian authorities. European and American sources sympathetic to the Armenians estimate that 600,000 Armenians died. Turkish sources put the deaths at 300,000 and maintain that at least as many Turks and other Muslims were slaughtered – not to mention half a million Central Asian Turks massacred by Russian troops before the Russian Revolution.

Yaver Hayri Paşa, a senior Turkish officer in the Medina in 1918. (Askeri Müzesi, Istanbul)

An Ottoman Army cookhouse on the Gallipoli front, 1915. This is clearly an Arab unit, one of those which played a significant role in the Turkish victory at Gallipoli. The large stew-pot is remarkably similar to those used by the famous Janissaries earlier in Ottoman history, and which became as much a focus of unit loyalty as the ancient Roman legionary eagles had done.

Kurds

To a great extent intermingled with the Christian Armenians were the Muslim Kurds who had a tradition of resistance to central government control. At this time they had little sense of Kurdish 'nationalism' but had developed a deep antagonism to their more advanced Armenian neighbours. In 1891 Sultan Abdülhamit raised a force of mostly Kurdish but also Turcoman and Arab tribal auxiliaries which came to be known as the *Hamidiye* cavalry. This was intended to counter Russia's famous Cossacks, and control the eastern parts of Anatolia. After 1908, however, the *Hamidiye* dispersed until, around 1914, a military commission started planning a new force from the same sources to be known as the *Asiret Hafif Süvari Alayları* or 'Tribal Light Cavalry'. It was supposed to consist of 24 regiments in four brigades. Service was to be between the ages of 18 and 45: three years as a recruit, twelve years as a trooper, twelve years in the reserve. All units were be commanded by regular cavalry officers while tribal chiefs would be given proper training in regular regiments before being commissioned as majors in the *Asiret Hafif Süvari Alayları*. Arms and uniforms would be supplied by the government but men had to find their own horses and harness. It remains unclear how far this new organization actually developed during the war, but between 20,000 and 30,000 tribal cavalry were already in the field against the Russian Army by the end of 1914. The importance of Kurdish irregular auxiliaries may actually have increased as regular Ottoman units were scattered across so many distant fronts.

The Caucasus

The Ottoman Army could rely on the support of Turkish-speaking Muslims in the Russian-ruled

Kurdish Irregulars in the Darsin/Tunçeli area of eastern Anatolia in 1917. Only officers in the Kurdish irregular Asiret Hafif Süvari Alayari auxiliary cavalry appear to have worn uniforms, their men being dressed in traditional Kurdish costume though armed by the state. The officer seated on the right wears the broad-brimmed 'sou'wester' seen on other Turkish cavalrymen. He also has a long-bladed sword from the Caucasus mountains on his hip. (Askeri Müzesi, Istanbul)

Military band playing on the parade ground at Damascus during a military review in April 1917. The band again wear Arab kufiya *headcloths and there are musical or medical symbols on their collar patches. (Imperial War Museum Q98412)*

Caucasus. Traditional antagonism between Sunni and Shia Muslims was disappearing in the wake of massacres by Russians and their Armenian auxiliaries. Local volunteers played a particularly important role on the extreme left flank of the Ottoman front, in the mountainous Artvin area near the Black Sea. Later in the war the Ottoman Army also tried to fill its depleted ranks by enlisting Turks from the Russian Caucasus but the main military contribution of these people was in the 'Islam Army' raised in Azarbayjan after the Russian Revolution. This drew in non-Ottoman Muslims from throughout the Caucasus and operated largely independently, just like similar forces raised by Georgia and Armenia. Though never officially recognized by the Ottoman government, the 'Islam Army' was given considerable help. Many Turkish Ottoman officers volunteered to serve in its ranks, the most famous being Enver's brother Nuri Paşa. As early as 1916 a Georgian Volunteer Legion had been raised, largely from the Muslim Georgian area of Lazistan, to fight alongside the Ottoman Army. Originally intended to promote a revolt in Russian-held Georgia, this Volunteer Legion remained under German control while the Ottomans wanted to use it as a normal battalion. In the end it took very little part in the fighting, being stationed on the Black Sea coast at Giresun until disbanded in January 1917.

Balkan Muslims

Other assorted forces lacking permanent or official Army structures were raised during the war, often being known as *müretteb* units. Another group of irregulars were the *fedais* who, mostly being of Balkan Muslim refugee origin, had been raised during and since the disastrous Balkan War. Often motivated by religious zeal or a desire for vengeance on the Balkan Christians, they were consequently regarded as fanatics by their foes. Thousands more were recruited in 1914, many being sent to the Caucasus front and north-western Iran in an effort to stimulate anti-Russian revolts there. Several hundred were also reported in Syria in late 1914. Later in the war the Ottomans again tried to recruit from the remaining Turkish population in Macedonia following the Austro-German-Bulgarian occupation of this area, though with little success.

Persia

Iran, or Persia as it was then known, was one of the most anarchic areas of the Middle East in 1914. Though independent in theory, it had been divided into British and Russian spheres of influence. Whereas the army of the Ottoman Empire could fight on half a dozen fronts and keep various numerically superior foes at bay, and Afghanistan could rely on its rugged terrain and warlike people to dissuade invaders, the Iranians had few such advantages. Efforts had been made to create a properly equipped regular army but all failed to produce lasting results. By 1914 some 13,000 infantry were scattered about the country, unpaid, untrained, badly clothed and led by an officer corps of staggering incompetence and corruption. The 38,000 or so cavalry were rather more effective, being recruited on a tribal basis under their own leaders, but even they formed little more than local militias defending only their own areas. Irregular cavalry were drawn from the Kurds, Lurs, Turcomans and Arabs though rarely from the majority Farsi (Persian) community, and such forces owed loyalty to their tribal leaders rather than to a central government. The artillery arm had 5–6,000 men with about 50 breech-loading guns, plus twice as many muzzle-loading field and mountain guns, only half of which were fit for service.

Two other military forces played a role greater than their numbers would suggest. One was the Russian-officered Persian Cossack Brigade which consisted of a little over 3,500 men in four cavalry regiments, four infantry companies, one horse and two mountain artillery batteries plus a machine-gun detachment. With modern equipment, discipline and training it was by far the best military force in pre-war Iran. Unfortunately it also suffered from confused loyalties, serving as an instrument of Russian influence and never being allowed to endanger Russian military domination. The second 'modern' force was the so-called Swedish Gendarmerie which had been reorganized by Swedish mercenary officers in 1911. It now consisted of six regiments, about 6,000 horsemen and infantry armed with Mauser rifles, mostly recruited from the Persian-speaking population. Unfortunately its Persian officers disliked their over-enthusiastic Swedish colleagues while the entire force suffered from the hostility of Russia and of the Persian Cossacks. As a result the Swedish Gendarmerie had developed pro-German sympathies.

Prey to internal dissension and foreign manipulation, Iran was clearly not in a position to defend itself when invaded by Russian, Ottoman and British forces during the Great War. In fact widespread anti-Russian feeling lay behind strong pro-Ottoman sympathies during the early part of the war. In November 1915 anti-Russian feelings ran so high that the Swedish Gendarmerie turned on the Persian Cossacks, forcing those in Hamadan to surrender. Interestingly enough the Gendarmerie were helped by a band of German and Austro-Hungarian POWs who had escaped from Russian camps in the Caucasus and Central Asia. Ottoman and German involvement in Iran was nevertheless often in competition. The Ottomans, for example, tried to organize a new Iranian army under a Persian General, Nizam al Saltaneh, who hoped to drive both the Russians and the British from his country. But this rudimentary force collapsed when the Russian Army in north-western Iran suddenly advanced south, its few infantry battalions simply deserting before the Russians arrived.

The Germans also set up their own puppet Persian government and army at Kermanshah, which in turn led to increased British intervention in southern Iran. In January 1916 a new pro-Russian government in Iran tried to reduce the numbers of Swedish Gendarmerie and increase those of the Persian Cossacks, the latter being placed under Russian control while the Russian Army moved to occupy a large part of western Iran. This did not, however, end pro-Ottoman sentiments in the area and as late as 1917 the Jangali tribe under Kuchik Khan attempted to stop an Anglo-Russian army marching through their forested mountain homeland south of the Caspian Sea. One of the few positive results of this confusion was the training of a handful of Persian officers by the Ottoman Air Force at Yesilköy near Istanbul. Since their own country had no aircraft, two of these men subsequently served as observers in the Ottoman 14th Squadron in 1918.

Ottoman Army camel transport on the Iraqi front in 1916. No beast of burden could operate as effectively in the desert as a single-humped dromedary or Arabian camel. This was well-known to the Turks, though their British foes took some time to relearn the lesson. (Askeri Müzesi, Istanbul)

Into this real-life version of John Buchan's 'Great Game' rode a number of Turkish, German and Austrian agents, the most effective being Dr. Wassmuss the one-time German Consul at Bushire. With his colleagues he organized tribal forces in many regions, damaging not only British and Russian influence but threatening a full-scale rising. The king of Afghanistan managed to control the excesses of the most fanatical anti-British elements but Britain still feared that Dr. Wassmuss aimed at India itself. The most successful period for these agents was 1915 and as a result mutually hostile bands of tribesmen and their mentors were soon chasing each other around much of Iran, Afghanistan and over the border into what is now Pakistan.

Somaliland, Eritrea and Ethiopia

While Germans, Austrians and Ottomans were stirring up trouble for the British in and beyond Iran, the Ottomans also stoked the embers of anti-colonial resentment against British, French and Italian forces in the Horn of Africa. The man at the centre of this trouble was Muhammad Abdullah Hasan, a resistance leader and poet who, known to his foes as the 'Mad Mullah', was neither mad nor a *Mullah* (religious teacher). Sayyid Muhammad Hasan, as he was more properly called, led his first rebellion against British rule in 1899 and by the outbreak of the Great War, British authority reached no further than the walls of a few coastal towns. But in November 1914 the British went on to the offensive while to the south, in what had recently become Italian Somaliland, there was also a build-up of troops, many drawn from Italian-ruled Eritrea.

The third Empire to be ruling Somali peoples was that of Ethiopia but in the immediate pre-war years this Christian kingdom was having its own internal problems. A new Emperor named Lij Jasu had come to the throne in 1913 and was attempting to reverse a thousand years of Christianity in Ethiopia by pursuing a pro-Islamic policy. In 1915 he became a Muslim and opened negotiations with the 'Mad Mullah' Sayyid Muhammad Hasan. Many also declared Lij Jasu to be mad but in fact he was a shrewd politician who hoped to win Ottoman military support to crush the rebellious Ethiopian nobility. Lij Jasu sent the Ottoman Sultan an Ethiopian flag bearing a crescent and Quranic declaration of faith,

Said Idris, a pro-Turkish military leader in Iran, 1916. His uniform is virtually identical to that of a very senior Ottoman Turkish officer. (Askeri Müzesi, Istanbul)

placed himself beneath the religious – though not political – authority of Istanbul and began recruiting an army in the largely Muslim southern lowlands. Fearing a mass rising the three European colonial powers sent extra troops to their respective colonies. In the end, though, it was the Ethiopians themselves who ended Lij Jasu's ambitions. In September 1916 the leading *Rases* or nobles of Shoa marched on Addis Ababa and, with the support of the Ethiopian Church, deposed Lij Jasu who fled to the wild coastal territory of the Danakil. Ethiopian troops subsequently took part in operations against Sayyid Muhammad Hasan's 'Dervishes', winning a bloody victory in August 1917.

Meanwhile the Ottoman consul at Harar, Mazar Bey, had been serving as Sayyid Muhammad Hasan's main contact with the outside world, particularly with General Ali Sait Paşa who commanded Ottoman forces in Yemen. In 1917 the General declared Sayyid Muhammad Hasan to be the Ottoman-approved governor of all Somalia. By that time, however, the Arab Revolt prevented Ottoman forces in Yemen from giving practical help, aside from a few Mauser and captured French Lebel rifles that were smuggled to the Somalis in return for food supplies.

Sources

Ahmad Emin (Yalman), *Turkey in the World War* (Newhaven 1930)
G.M. Bayliss, *Operations in Persia 1914–1919* (reprint London 1987)
T.N. Barker, *Double Eagle and Crescent* (New York 1957)
A. Djemal Paşa, *Memoirs of a Turkish Statesman, 1913–1919* (1922)
Sayed Ali El-Edroos, *The Hashemite Arab Army 1908–1979* (Amman & London 1980)
H. Kannengeisser, *The Campaign in Gallipoli* (1927)
Lord Kinross, *Ataturk, The Rebirth of a Nation* (London 1964)
K. Klinghardt, *Denkwürdigkeiten des Marschalls Izzet Pascha* (Leipzig 1927)
M. Larcher, *La Guerre Turque dans la Guerre Mondiale* (Paris 1926)
A. Moorhead, *Gallipoli* (London 1956)
C.C.R. Murphy, *Soldiers of the Prophet* (London 1927)
C.C.R. Murphy, 'The Turkish Army in the Great War', *Journal of the Royal United Services Institute* LXV (1920) pp. 90–104
R. de Nogales, *Four Years beneath the Crescent* (1926)
J. Pomiankowski, *Der Zusammenbruch des Ottomanischen Reiches* (Leipzig, Zürich, Vienna 1928)
O. Liman von Sanders, *Five Years in Turkey* (Annapolis 1927)
U. Trumpener, *Germany and the Ottoman Empire 1914–1918* (Princeton 1968)
J.L. Wallach, *Anatomie einer Militärhilfe* (Düsseldorf 1976)
War Office, *Handbook of the Turkish Army* (Cairo 1915)

Turkish Army nurses in 1915. Their uniforms are basically the same as those of European nurses except for their head-cloths which, under Islamic law, had to cover the hair entirely. (Askeri Müzesi, Istanbul)

THE PLATES

A: Senior officers and ceremonial
A1: Mustafa Kemal Bey, General Staff service dress, 1915

Mustafa Kemal, who later adopted the family name of Atatürk, is shown here in the uniform he wore during the Gallipoli campaign. Although a colonel attached to the General Staff he wears a uniform typical of most field officers. This includes that most characteristic item of First World War Turkish military costume, the *kabalak*, a hat formed of a strip of fabric wound around a semi-stiff frame. *Kabalaks* could be wound in various ways, but the one worn here was the most common. He also wears the Imtiyaz (distinguished service) medal, the Liyakat (merit) medal and the ribbon of the Turkish War Medal twice. His pistol is probably a Mauser M.1910/14.

A2: Enver Paşa, dress uniform, c.1917

As Minister of War and Vice-Commander-in-Chief of the Ottoman Armed Forces, Enver Paşa wears the dress uniform of a general, though without the doubled red trouser stripes normal for generals. He also has a black lambskin *kalpak* hat. In addition to the Turkish Order of Osman, his medals include the Prussian Order of the Red Eagle with sash, the Prussian Order Pour le Mérite, the Prussian Iron Cross, the Bulgarian Order of Merit and the Austrian Military Cross of Merit.

A3: Standard bearer with regimental flag, Nişancı (Rifle) Battalion

Apart from the unusual loose winding of his *kabalak*, this standard bearer wears ordinary infantry uniform plus the olive-green collar patches worn only by sharp-shooter units. The visible side of the flag bears the Muslim Declaration of Faith: *La ilaha ill' Allah, wa Muhammad rasul Allah*, 'There is no god but God, and Muhammad is the Prophet of God'. The other side of the flag bore the Ottoman Empire's coat of arms.

B: Infantry
B1: Turkish line infantryman, marching order, c.1914

The ordinary Turkish infantryman of 1914 was well equipped and well dressed. Only when large numbers of reserves were called up did the standard of uniforms deteriorate. This man carries full marching equipment, as he might have appeared at the start of the Great War. While his simple but practical uniform is purely Turkish, the rest of his equipment is German in style. He is armed with a 'Turkish' (meaning made specifically for the Ottoman Turkish Army) Mauser rifle M.1893. By 1918 a variety of different rifles were also in use.

B2: Infantryman, off duty, Galicia c.1917

This man has been almost entirely re-equipped by the Austrians or Germans and has been issued with a captured Russian Mossin-Nagant M.1891 rifle. His tunic is one of several much cruder patterns introduced during the course of the war. Note the strengthening patches added on the knees and elbows. Towards the end of the war a variety of different, and perhaps locally made, cartridge belts were also in use. Surviving photographs show that the old-fashioned soft red fez, supposedly phased out before the Great War started, was sometimes still worn when men were off duty.

B3: Arab bicycle infantry, Arabia 1915

At the start of the First World War a large proportion of the Ottoman Armies in Syria and Iraq were recruited from the local Arab populations. They fought with distinction at Gallipoli but many later joined the Arab Revolt and fought as allies of the British. Others remained loyal to the Ottoman Empire until the end of the war. Most were uniformed and equipped in the same way as Turkish infantry, except that they wore the Arab *kufiya* headcloth and *'aqal* camel hair ring instead of the Turkish *kabalak* hat. But some wore white uniforms like this man stationed in the Muslim Holy City of Medina. He is armed with the German M.1888 rifle. There were supposed to be four cyclists in each infantry battalion at the start of the war; but the only other complete bicycle-mounted unit in the Ottoman Army was an infantry company far away at Edirne near the Bulgarian border.

C: Cavalry
C1: Cavalry officer

The most notable feature of this man's uniform is the very large form of *kabalak* with upturned brim and a long rear part to shade his neck. Otherwise his dress is

A Turkish officer and his African batman in Libya, 1918. The bridle, saddle and stirrups of the officer's horse are of a typical North African or Libyan type. Ottoman Turkish and Libyan Arab guerilla forces maintained their resistance throughout the war, effectively penning the invading Italians against the coast. (Askeri Müzesi, Istanbul)

that of a typical Ottoman officer. He carries an M.1909 cavalry sabre with the Turkish crescent and star cut through its guard. On his chest he wears the ribbon of the Turkish War Medal.

C2: NCO of a Turkish cavalry regiment, c.1917
The cavalryman's saddle and harness are essentially the same as the officer's, though non-commissioned ranks had to carry more equipment. This man wears a cavalry version of the Turkish *kabalak*. (Arab cavalry units were similarly dressed except for their *kufiya* head-cloths.) The grey collar patches identify him as a cavalryman and on his back he carries a 'Turkish' Mauser M.1905 cavalry carbine. Turkish cavalry horses were generally tough but small ponies, often better able to cope with harsh Middle Eastern terrain though less formidable in a charge.

C3: Kurdish irregular officer
The Ottoman Empire's auxiliary cavalry consisted of tribal auxiliaries, mostly recruited among the Kurds of eastern Anatolia. Uniforms were supposed to be provided by the government, but available photographs indicate that even some officers still wore traditional Kurdish costume. This man does, however, have a Turkish Army greatcoat and boots. The rest of his clothes, and his probably Martini rifle, are his own.

D: Specialist troops
D1: Assault party, 1918
Towards the end of the Great War some Ottoman infantry were issued with steel helmets which differed from the German type in several respects. Among the first units to be so equipped were 'stormtroopers', comparable to those seen on the European fronts; these served in Palestine and in Transcaucasia. Over his left shoulder this man carries a bag of grenades and he is armed with the German rather than 'Turkish' Mauser M.1898 rifle. This may suggest that he was attached to the recently formed Yıldırım Army in Syria and Palestine.

D2: Ski-troops NCO, Caucasus c.1917
Turkish formations of ski-troops evolved under Austrian or German direction and reflected Austro-German mountain troops. This man is well equipped for the rigours of an eastern Anatolian winter

Turkish ski-troops wearing complete white snow-camouflage, including gauze screens across their faces, 1915. They would probably operate as snipers. (Askeri Müzesi, Istanbul)

campaign. His skis have simple foot or ankle bindings rather than the modern form of boot clips, and he uses only a single ski pole. Photographs of Turkish ski-troops show some with very light-coloured collar patches. These have been hypothetically shown as white on this reconstruction.

D3: Officer of a machine-gun detachment
Beneath his long overcoat this officer would wear a uniform similar to that of Mustafa Kemal in Plate A1, although his *kabalak* is different in both shape and winding. Only officers wore this style, though not all of them did so. The grass-green collar indicates his branch of the service and is repeated in the narrow edging of the cloth around his *kabalak*. The man is also armed with a revolver, probably of Austrian manufacture.

E: Artillery
E1: Artillery officer, Gallipoli 1915
Some Turkish artillerymen continued to wear white uniforms in summer, as Ottoman troops had done for almost a century. This officer also wears a *kabalak* with blue edging indicating his branch of service, and with its leather chin-strap pushed up on top. On his hip is a large artillery-type Parabellum pistol in its holster.

E2: Artillery officer, Galicia

Although the units that the Ottoman Empire sent to Galicia were well equipped and generally uniformed in the usual fashion, they were often resupplied by their German or Austrian allies. The leather braces to this man's belt also appear to have been characteristic of the Galician front. He wears a standard officer's uniform, his branch of service being shown by his blue collar, and he has the ribbon of the Turkish War Medal.

E3: Artillery Sergeant, Galicia

This NCO is basically dressed in the standard uniform for his rank, which is indicated by both shoulder markings and rings on his sleeves. His tunic and trousers are once more of a very rough and poorly made type seen later in the war.

F: Air Forces

F1: Naval Pilot Engineer Mülazım (Lieutenant) Ahmet of the Naval Flying School, Yeşilköy, dress uniform.

Most Ottoman aircrew were recruited from the Turkish heartland or from Turkish or other Muslim refugees from the Balkans; others came from the Arab provinces of the Ottoman Empire as far south as Yemen, or even from neutral Iran. Captain Ahmet was of Arab-African origin and may have been the first 'black' Air Force pilot in aviation history, having received his 'wings' in 1914–15. He wears the standard dress uniform of an Ottoman naval officer, although as a technical officer the rings on his sleeves lack the loops worn by combat officers. The scarlet between the rings also identifies him as an engineer.

F2: Army Air Force Observer Mülazım (Lieutenant) Sıtkı, No. 4 Squadron, southern Anatolia 1917

Lt. Sıtkı was a Turkish officer who qualified as an observer at Yeşilköy outside Istanbul in 1917. He first served on the southern coast of Turkey, then in what is now Jordan and finally in southern Syria against Lawrence of Arabia and the Arab Revolt. Here he wears the full uniform of an Ottoman flyer, distinguished by his red collar, the winged device on his *kalpak* and the Air Force badge on his left breast. The flying coat, helmet and goggles he carries are all of German make.

F3: German volunteer Pilot Kleinehayk of No. 10 Squadron, southern Anatolia, summer 1917

Kleinehayk was a German reserve officer seconded to the Turkish Air Force, where he served for several months in 1917. Here he wears a *kabalak* with Turkish Air Force wings on the front. He is also shown with a German 13–18 cm aerial camera.

G: Navy

G1: Sailor of naval landing party

The overwhelming might of the British and French

Ottoman Army medical orderlies with a 'cacolet', or camel litter, in 1916. Such litters were also used by Allied armies in the Middle East and though excruciatingly uncomfortable were often the only means of evacuating the wounded. Note the large Red Crescent arm-bands worn by one orderly and the officer. (Askeri Müzesi, Istanbul)

The funeral of Sultan Resat in Istanbul in 1918. The cortège is escorted by troops from the palace guard wearing white lambskin kalpaks with plumes at the front. Other photographs show that the route of the funeral was guarded by men from the Istanbul Fire Brigade, itself a regular Army unit. (Askeri Müzesi, Istanbul)

navies meant that large Turkish ships could almost never venture into the Aegean or Mediterranean Seas, though they were active against the Russians in the Black Sea. Instead the Turkish Navy concentrated on small coastal operations against enemy (and pirate) bases on islands off the Anatolian coast. Here a petty officer with such a landing party wears the white summer uniform worn by all Turkish seamen, plus a distinctive white *kabalak*. On his legs he has canvas gaiters over stiff canvas boots with leather soles.

G2: Naval able seaman
British influence was widespread throughout the modernized Ottoman Turkish Navy: Turkish ships were painted in the same colours as those of the Royal Navy. Naval uniforms of men and officers reflected British influence and officer insignia also mirrored that of the Royal Navy. Only the shape and design of this sailor's cap is distinctly Turkish for, like the Ottoman officer's peakless hat worn by Naval Pilot Ahmet (Plate F1), it lacks any protuberance which would prevent a Muslim's forehead from touching the ground as he prayed.

G3: Naval Commander, winter uniform 1915
The fact that this senior naval officer still wears an old-fashioned stiff form of red fez, supposedly phased out when the Ottoman Navy was modernized, might suggest that he was a member of the naval reserve. The Commodore's three rings and loop on his sleeves are virtually identical to those of the Royal Navy. Meanwhile his leather boots and gaiters suggest that he has a shore posting.

H: Miscellaneous
H1: Istanbul Fire Brigade Infantryman
The Istanbul Fire Brigade constituted a regular Army infantry regiment. When serving in that capacity its uniform was identical to that of other infantry regiments except for a special collar badge. This man is shown in his fireman's uniform which has the same collar badges, including the Arabic number 12 which might refer to his fire station in Istanbul.

H2: Allied Afghan Prince, c.1917
Among the many Muslim nations where the Ottoman Empire tried to foment anti-British, anti-Russian, anti-French and anti-Italian risings was Afghanistan, which was at that time under a large degree of British control. In 1917 a delegation of pro-Ottoman Afghan leaders visited Istanbul where they met senior military officers at the Flying School at Yesilköy. The very Ottoman-style uniforms worn by a prince in this delegation suggests that they had travelled incognito from Afghanistan, and were given suitable clothes when they arrived.

H3: Boy soldier, volunteer bomb thrower at Gallipoli, 1915
Under the Ottoman conscription system a son sometimes served in place of his father. Such youngsters often fought hard and could become NCOs. This boy is a sergeant, as shown by his shoulder-boards. The slippers on his feet might indicate that the Army had no boots small enough or that his military role necessitated stealth.

Notes sur les planches en couleurs

A Officiers de haut grade et Cérémonial. A1 Mustafa Kemal dans son uniforme de la campagne de Gallipoli. Il porte un uniforme typique d'officier sur le terrain dont le chapeau kabalak distinctif. Son pistolet est sans doute un Mauser Modèle 1910–14. **A2** Enver Pasa, Ministre de la Guerre, porte l'uniforme de service d'un Général sans les doubles rayures rouges standard sur le pantalon. L'ordre prussien de l'Aigle Rouge avec ceinture en tissu, la Croix de fer prussienne, l'Ordre prussien Pour le Mérite, l'Ordre bulgarien du Mérite et la Croix militaire autrichienne du Mérite. **A3** Porte-étendard portant un kabalak lâche et les écussons vert olive d'un tireur d'élite. Le drapeau qu'il porte comporte la Déclaration de Foi musulmane.

B Infanterie. B1 Fantassin vers 1914 avec kit de marche complet. Son uniforme est turc mais le reste do son kit est de style allemand. Le fusil est un Mauser M1893 'turc' conçu spécialement pour l'armée turque ottomane. **B2** Le fez rouge mour indique que ce soldat, autour de 1917, n'est pas en service. Ré-éuipé par les autrichiens ou les allemands, il a un fusil Mossin-Nagent. Sa tunique est de modèle plus simple, introduit pendant la guerre. **B3** Soldat arabe d'infanterie à bicyclette, Arabie, 1915. Il porte un foulard et un bandeau en poil de chameau arabes au lieu de kabalak turc et porte un fusil allemand M1888.

C Cavalerie. C1 Officier de cavalerie portant un uniforme typique d'officier ottoman, bien que son kabalak soit paritculièrement grand. Il porte un sabre de cavalerie modèle 1909 avec un croissant et une étoile turcs incisés sur sa garde. **C2** Régiment turc de cavalerie NCO autour de 1917 porte un kabalak de cavalerie. Il a les écussons de col gris d'un membre de la cavalerie et porte une carabine de cavalerie Mauser 'turque' M1905. **C3** Officier irrégulier Kurde. Il porte un manteau et des bottes de l'armée turque, le reste de ses vêtement et son fusil Martini lui appartiennent sans doute.

D Troupes spécialisées. Détachement d'assaut, 1918. **D1** Cet homme porte un casque en acier, il a un sac de grenades et est armé d'un fusil Mauser allemand plutôt que 'turc' M1898. **D2** Troupes NCO à ski du Caucase autour de 1917. Ses skis ont des fixations rudimentaires et il a un seul bâton. **D3** Officier de détachement de mitrailleuses. Porte un long manteau. Il porte un kabalak de style officier et son col vert indique sa branche de service. Il est armé d'un révolver.

E Artillerie. E1 Officier d'artillerie, Gallipoli 1915. Porte un uniforme blanc comme les troupes ottomanes l'avaient fait traditionnellement durant l'été. Son kabalak est bordé de bleu, ce qui indique sa branche de service. Il porte un gros pistolet Parabellum d'artillerie dans son étui. **E2** Officier d'artillerie, Galicie, qui porte l'uniforme d'officier standard. Sa branche de service est indiquée par son col bleu et il a le ruban de la Médaille de guerre turque. **E3** Sergent d'artillerie, Galicie, en uniforme standard de son rang, indiqué par des marques à l'épaule et des passepoils autour de ses manches. Sa tunique et son pantalon sont de la qualité moindre qui fut utilisée plus tard durant la guerre.

F Forces de l'air. F1 Le capitaine Ahmet, étant donné son origine africaine, fut l'un des premiers pilotes 'nores' de l'histoire de l'aviation. Il porte l'uniforme standard d'un officier naval ottoman. Les passepoils sur ses manches indiquent qu'il est officier technique et la couleur écarlate entre les passepoils indique qu'il est ingénieur. **F2** Le Lt. Sitki porte l'uniforme complet d'un aviateur ottoman. Sa veste de pilote, ses lunettes et son casque sont fabriqués en Allemagne. **F3** Officier allemand de réserve détaché à l'armée aérienne turque. Il a un kabalak avec des ailes à l'avant et une caméra aérienne allemande 13–18cm.

G Marine. G1 Sous-officier d'une compagnie de débarquement qui porte un uniforme blanc d'été, un kabalak blanc et des guêtres de toile sur des bottes de toile raide à semelle de cuir. **G2** Ce matelot de la marine ottomane. Ce modèle garantissait que lien ne puisse empêcher le front musulman de toucher le sol durant ses prières. **G3** Ce commandant naval en uniforme d'hiver porte une forme raide démodée de fez rouge. Les bottes et les jambières en cuir suggèrent qu'il a un poste à terre.

H Divers. H1 Soldat d'infanterie des Pompiers d'Istambul. L'uniforme est identique à celui d'autres régiments d'infanterie sauf pour le badge spécial au col. **H2** Prince afghan allié autour de 1917. Le Prince porte un uniforme de style ottoman indiquant qu'il a peut-être voyagé incognito depuis l'Afghanistan. **H3** Les épaulettes plates de l'uniforme de ce garçon indiquent qu'il est un sergent. Il porte des pantoufles soit parce que l'Armée n'avait pas de bottes suffisamment petites pour lui, soit parce qu'il devait travailler à la dérobée.

Farbtafeln

A Offiziere höheren Rangs und Zeremoniell. **A1** Mustafa Kemal in seiner Gallipoli-Felduniform. Er trägt die typische Uniform eines Stabsoffiziers mit dem charakteristischen Kabalak-Hut. Bei seiner Pistole handelt es sich wahrscheinlich um eine Mauser, Modell 1910–14. **A2** Der Kriegsminister Enver Pasa trägt die Dienstuniform eines Generals ohne die standardmäßigen doppelten roten Streifen an den Hosen. Der preußische Orden des Roten Adlers mit Schärpe, das preußische Eiserne Kreuz, der preußische Orden Pour le Mérite, der bulgarische Verdienstorden und das österreichische Militärdienstkreuz. **A3** Standartenträger mit einem lose gebundenen Kabalak und dem olivgrünen Aufnäher der Scharfschützen. Auf der Flagge, die er trägt, steht das islamische Glaubensbekenntnis geschrieben.

B Infanterie. **B1** Feldinfanterist um 1914 in voller Marshausrüstung. Seine Uniform ist türkischer Herkunft, doch der Rest seiner Ausrüstung ist dem Stil nach deutsch. Beim Gewehr handelt es sich um eine 'türkische' Mauser M1893, die eigens für die osmanisch-türkische Armee entworfen wurde. **B2** Am weichen, roten Fes erkennt man, daß dieser Soldat, ca. 1917, außer Dienst ist. Er wurde von den Österreichern oder den Deutschen neu ausgerüstet und hat ein russisches Mossin-Nagent-Gewehr. Seine Uniformjacke entspricht dem gröberen Modell, das während des Krieges eingeführt wurde. **B3** Arabischer Soldat der Fahrrad-Infanterie, Arabien, 1915.Anstelle des türkischen Kabalak trägt er die arabische Kopfbedeckung mit Kamelhaarschnüren und hat ein deutsches Gewehr M1888.

C Kavallerie. **C1** Kavallerieoffizier in der typisch osmanischen Offiziersuniform, wobei sein Kabalak ungewöhnlich groß ist. Er hat einen Kavalleriesäbel des 1909er Modells, auf dem der türkische Halbmond und Stern auf dem Stichblatt eingraviert ist. **C2** Unteroffizier des türkischen Kavallerieregiments, ca. 1917, im Kavallerickabalak. Er hat graue Kragenstücke eines Kavalleristen und hat 'türkischen' Mauser-Kavalleriekarabiner M1905 bei sich. **C3** Kurdischer Freischärler-Offizier. Er trägt einen Mantel und Stiefel der türkischen Armee, der Rest seiner Kleidung und sein Martini-Gewehr gehören wahrscheinlich ihm selbst.

D Sondertruppen. Strumtruppe, 1918 **D1** Dieser Mann trägt einen Stahlhelm, hat eine Tasche mit Granaten bei sich und ist mit einer deutschen anstatt einer 'türkischen' Mauser M1898 bewaffnet. **D2** Unteroffizier der Skitruppe, ca. 1917 im Kaukasus. Seine Skier haben eine einfache Bindung, und er benutzt einen einzelnen Skistock. **D3** Offizier eines Mashinengewehrkommandos. Er trägt einen langen Mantel. Er trägt einen Kabalak im Offizierstil und sein grüner Kragen gibt seine Truppengattung an. Er ist mit einem Revolver bewaffnet.

E Artellerie. **E1** Artellerie-Offizer, Gallipoli 1915. Er trägt die weiße Uniform, wie sie die osmanischen Truppen traditionsgemäß im Sommer trugen. Sein Kabalak hat eine blaue Randeinfassung, die seine Truppengattung bezeichnet. Er trägt eine große Parabellum-Pistole des Artellerietyps in der Pistolentasche. **E2** Artellerie-Offizier, Galizien, in der standardmäßigen Offiziersuniform. Seine Truppengattung wird durch den blauen Kragen angegeben, und der trägt das Band der türkischen Kriegsmedaille. **E3** Artellerie-Feldwebel, Galizien, in der Standaruniform seines Rangs, der durch die Schulterstücke und die Streifen am Ärmel bezeichnet ist. Seine Uniformjacke und die Hosen sind aus dem relativ schlechten Stoff, der in den späteren Kriegsjahren auftauchte.

F Luftwaffe. **F1** Hauptmann Ahmet, der arabisch-afrikanischer Abstammung war, war einer der ersten 'schwarzen' Piloten in der Geschichte der Luftfahrt. Er trägt den standardmäßigen Dienstanzug eines osmanischen Marineoffiziers. Die Streifen an seinen Ärmeln kennzeichnen ihn als technischen Offizier und die scharlachrote Farbe zwischen den Ringen deutet an, daß er Ingenieur ist. **F2** Lt. Sitki trägt die komplette Uniform eines osmanischen Fliegers, sein Fleigermantel, die Fliegerbrille und der Helm sind deutscher Luftwaffe überstellt, trägt einen Kabalak mit dem Pilotenabzeichen an der Vorderseite und ein deutsches 13–18 cm Luftbildgerät.

G Marine. **G1** Maat eines Landungstrupps in weißer Sommeruniform, einem weißen Kabalak und Segeltuchgamaschen über steifen Stiefeln mit Ledersohlen. **G2** Dieser Vollmatrose trägt die charakteristische schildlose Mütze der osmanischen Marine. Durch diese Form war es den Moslems möglich, mit der Stirn beim Gebet ungehindert den Boden zu berühren. **G3** Dieser Marinekommandeur in der Winteruniform trägt eine altmodische, steife Form des roten Fes. Die Lederstiefel und Gamaschen legen nahe, daß er an Land postiert ist.

H Diverses. **H1** Infanterist der Istanbuler Feuerwehr. Die Uniform gleicht abgesehen vom besonderen Kragenabzeichen der der anderen Infanterieregimenter. **H2** Allierter afghanischer Prinz, ca. 1917. Der Prinz trägt eine Uniform osmanischen Stils, was wahrscheinlich bedeutet, daß er inkognito aus Afghanistan angereist ist. **H3** Die Schulterstücke an der Uniform dieses Jungen kennziechnen ihn als Sergeanten. Er trägt Pantoffeln und zwar entweder, weil die Armee keine Stiefel hatte, die klein genug waren, oder weil er bei seinem Auftrag schleichen mußte.